MAXIMS *From* MAHABHARATA

INDICA

ISBN 979-8-88555-441-1

MAXIMS
From
MAHABHARATA

SRIDHAR POTARAJU

INDICA

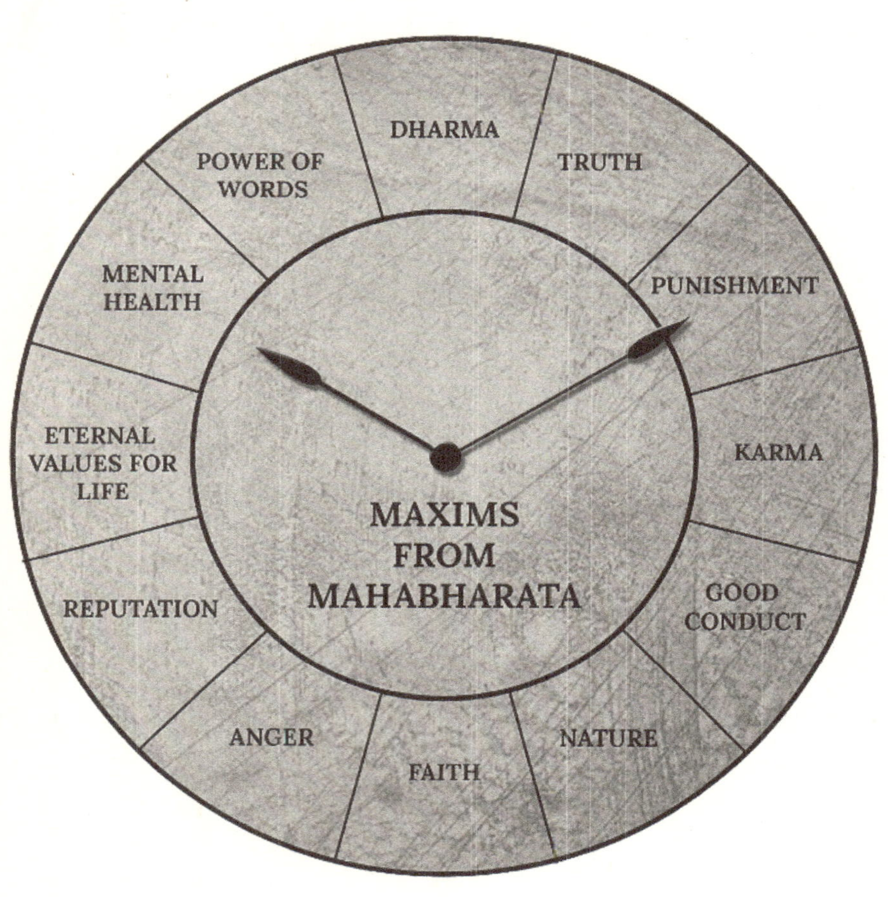

Design by Ms. PRANATI POTARAJU

अ आ इ ई उ ऊ ऋ ॠ

A ā I ī u ū ṛ ṝ

लृ ए ऐ ओ औ ◌ं ◌ः

lṛ e ai o au ṃ ḥ

क ख ग घ ङ

Ka kha ga gha ṅa

च छ ज झ ञ

Ca cha ja jha ña

ट ठ ड ढ ण

ṭa ṭha ḍa ḍha ṇa

त थ द ध न

Ta tha da dha na

प फ ब भ म

Pa pha ba bha ma

य र ल व

Ya ra la va

श ष स ह

Śa ṣa sa ha

Contents

Preface

Justice V. Ramasubramanian
Judge, Supreme Court of India

2, Akbar Road,
New Delhi-110011
Tel. : 011-23018043

PREFACE

At the outset, I deem it my duty to salute Shri Sridhar Potaraju, Advocate, for diving deep into the ocean of *Mahabharata* and bringing out pearls of wisdom in the form of *maxims*. While every other lawyer is attempting to master latin *maxims* for *"udara nimitham"* (*as Adhishankara called it*), Sridhar Potaraju has focused on *Mahabharata* which is considered as the 5th Veda (*Bharatah Panchamo Vedah*). The scholars have said that there is nothing in the world which is not there in the *Mahabharata* and that whatever is not there in the *Mahabharata* cannot be found elsewhere.

Another name for *Mahabharata* is *"victory"* (jaya)

Narayanam Namaskritya
Naram chaiva Narottamam
Deveem Saraswateem Vyassam
Tato Jayamudeerayet

It is the story of triumph of the good over the evil. But the most fascinating and astounding aspect of *Mahabharata* is that all characters in the epic story present a complex mixture of good and evil. In the *Ramayana, Dharma* stood on one side and *Adharma* stood pitted against it. But in *Mahabharata* all characters, with very few exceptions such as *Vidura* come out sometimes as nobel minded and at times as evil minded. *Vedavyasa,* the greatest of all sages has presented in this epic, the nuances of *Dharma* through innumerable characters. The beauty of this epic is that its author *Maharishi Vedavyasa* is also one of the characters, who fathers three central characters, namely, Dhritarashtra, Pandu and Vidura. In a way, the huge war that this epic speaks about, was one fought between two branches of his progenies.

One Maxim that keeps getting repeated in this epic is perhaps *"kalohi duratikramaḥ"* meaning no one can raise above the dictates of time.

Shri Sridhar Potaraju has grouped all the maxims found in the *Mahabharata* under 12 different headings. Every one of them is a gem. Therefore, the book on hand will be of immeasurable value for those who celebrate and value life here and life hereafter.

I whole heartedly congratulate Sridhar Potaraju for this excellent contribution to humanity.

(V. Ramasubramanian)

Acknowledgements

Daivam Manushya Rupēna, means *God through the medium of Human,* is something I personally experienced, particularly, in the journey of conceptualizing the thought of compiling Maxims from Indian sources. As and when I was stuck due to lack of vision or was unable to access the resources, I experienced an element of divine guidance through human agency holding my hand and guiding me ahead. I seek to acknowledge each and every one of them and for brevity, may not be able to name each.

The list of people I need to acknowledge can only start with my mother Smt. Daliparthy Ratnavali, a working woman who raised both sons and a daughter equally and my father Late P. Sreerama Rao, a self-made man, for inculcating in us the importance of living life with principles and discipline. My parents raised us 3 siblings- *Anna, Akka* and me, the youngest at home – by providing us access to modern education while keeping us grounded in our cultural and civilisational roots, for they understood that modern education without spirituality would not be sufficient to live a meaningful and contended life. We were never judged on our academic performance but were encouraged to work hard and discover ourselves.

I thank Hon'ble Justice V. Ramasubramanian for taking out his precious time to peruse my book and agreeing to give a preface.

I bow down in reverence to Sri. K. Parasaran, a scholar in Sanskrit and Indian Knowledge Systems as well as an eminent jurist who has blessed me with his time and valuable inputs during my journey of compiling the maxims. He has always granted me time to discuss the various aspects of this book and gave critical suggestions time and again.

I would like to further thank the following people without whose contribution, the book would not have been possible:

Ms. Ankita Sharma and Mr. Vishnu Thulasi Menon, my young Advocate friends for sparing their time liberally and assisting me in compiling the maxims.

Ms. Sanhita Jani Vyas, a passionate Sanskrit Teacher for patiently composing the Sanskrit verses and reading the Manuscript.

Ms. Aruna Gollamudi, an old friend who has painstakingly gone through the manuscript and given me candid feedback. I can only acknowledge her contribution with gratitude.

Ms. Naveena, my spouse and P.V. Ramana Kumar my older brother for being available as objective listeners encouraging me to go ahead with publishing the work. Pranati Potaraju for structuring the manuscript into a book form initially. Several friends, and colleagues at work for being there and supporting me in completing the book.

Sri Hari Kiran Vadlamani, Founder – Indica for reposing faith in my work and publishing this book.

Ms. Dhanya K, Senior Publishing Manager Notion Press Publishing for very patiently guiding me in my maiden attempt to bring out this book.

10.04.2022
New Delhi   Sridhar Potaraju

Story behind the Book

"The richness of the Sanskrit language is almost beyond belief. Many centuries ago that language contained words to describe states of the conscious, the subconscious and the unconscious mind and a variety of other concepts which have been evolved by modern psychology, psychoanalysis and psychotherapy. Further, it has many a word, of which there is no exact synonym even in the richest modern languages. That is why some of the most enlightened modern writers have been driven occasionally to use Sanskrit words when writing in English. Consider, for example, the following passage in Dr. Raynor Johnson's The Imprisoned Splendour"

"To facilitate discussion I propose to call this higher level buddhi (coming from a Sanskrit word meaning 'wisdom'). Buddhi apprehends Truth directly – fragments of truth only, of course. It offers no reason for its perceptions, but it makes no mistakes, and this wisdom is passed through the level of Mind, to be there clothed in intelligible form".

And the following words by J. Robert Oppenheimer in Einstein: A Centenary Volume:

"Einstein is also, and I think rightly, known as a man of very great goodwill and humanity. Indeed, if I had to think of a single word for his attitude towards human problems, I would pick the Sanskrit word Ahimsa, not to hurt, harmlessness."

– N.A. Palkhivala

India's Priceless Heritage

As a person who enjoyed play of words in conversations, I always found proverbs, similes, idioms very handy in a conversation. As they help one put across a point effectively using general phrases which are commonly understood. Our school had very good Telugu teachers Sri Murthy Sir and Smt. Kusuma Kumari teacher, who would use proverbs, idioms, similes liberally while teaching or discipling us in class. The syllabus had excerpts from Telugu literary works based on Ramayana and Mahabharata which highlighted eternal values through great personalities. Our language classes had effectively become source of learning eternal values without making them sound like a class on moral science, thanks to our teachers.

Further exposure to books of Palkhivala gave me an insight to the wealth of knowledge hidden in our ancient texts, all composed in Sanskrit. Most of the eminent persons with roots in Indian cultural milieu quote from Sanskrit works. The limitations of english language are exposed profoundly when Sanskrit works are translated into english, for vocabulary of every language is shaped by its cultural and civilisation roots with their inherent limitations.

I always believe that reading the original work is critical to forming an opinion independently, uninfluenced by the views of the commentators. In this process I started looking for and found the original works in Sanskrit with English translations. The journey was quiet exciting for simple reason that without formal training I was attempting to decipher the meaning of Sanskrit words and phrases using my language skills in Telugu and Hindi aided by English translation.

I found stories from Indian literature are a great source for imparting values. No wonder though on account of statistical literacy our nation may not be well placed but on Wisdom index, most of the Indians though illiterate would be found to be much wiser than the *literati* both on account of their common sense and sense of dharma. Primarily because of their natural exposure to our national epics i.e., Ramayana and Mahabharata passed on from times immemorial across the length and breadth of the country.

I started reading Valmiki Ramayana, followed it up with Mahabharata and the pursuit continues. While reading any book I inherited my father's habit of marking or writing my thoughts on the book. This habit made me mark several thoughts, ideas, maxims, words in these epics. The reading of these epics was spread over about 8 years commencing sometime in later half of 2012. I found various anecdotes which had subtle message on how to live in harmony with nature, society and one's own self. It was then that I started wondering as to how this wealth of knowledge can be shared with the current generation who are conditioned by English medium education to shrug off anything Indian as not being cool. But never the less in need of help but refusing to look at the original sources of wisdom.

Maxims in Latin entered my life when I joined Law. With my experience beginning as a Student of Law in 1994, I can safely say that in my generation or a generation before me none had access to Latin as a language. It was neither taught in Schools much less in Universities or in Law Schools. But that did not deter anyone nor made anyone resist these maxims. Infact, conversations amongst Law students would have these maxims as if they always lived with them.

I started noticing the stark absence of any reading material with Indian Maxims. India as world's oldest living civilization has contributed immensely to the world through its epics. However, the bridge between the Indian knowledge systems and their contemporary use continues and seems to be increasing. Having opportunity to live and interact with Indians from almost all parts of the Country only reinforced my belief that we should have a compilation of Maxims from Indian sources which have their roots in our soil, hence easy for all to relate to them. Infact, usage of Indian

Maxims in public discourse including in formal proceedings would make them more meaningful to one and all.

The idea of working on Indian Maxims occurred to me sometime during 2018 and has since grown sub-consciously. The unfortunate spread of pandemic and nationwide lockdown announced in last week of March suddenly left me with no routine or work. On 28th March 2020 the latent desire to compile Indian Maxims emerged as if, 'The Idea whose time had come'.

The lock down had left couple of young friends confined to their homes away from family and work. Both Ms. Ankita Sharma and Mr. Vishnu Thulasi Menon, both Post Graduates in Law and practicing Advocates, were very enthusiastic when I suggested that we can have a routine and start compiling maxims from Mahabharata which I had marked while reading over past few years from the 9 Volumes of Mahabharata published by Parimal Publication which had Sanskrit verses with English Translation. The work began with my reading out small stories, over conference calls, from Mahabharata and noting down some verses which could be compiled for the book. All 3 of us could read Devanagari but were not familiar with Sanskrit. But that did not deter us as we would read the translation and trace the relevant Sanskrit verse jointly adding our individual bits of language skills.

My mother tongue Telugu has strong roots in Sanskrit, which helped me in pronouncing Sanskrit words. It was a union of reading Devanagiri and processing it in Telugu to decipher the meaning aided by English translation. Time was available in abundance to undertake this task.

It started as an exercise to keep ourselves sane amidst the uncertainty all around, but soon became a daily work routine. We would connect on a group callon our mobiles everyday from 3 – 5.30 pm and make notes. This routine continued until June 2020 when professional work started with lockdown restrictions easing down marginally. By then we had together compiled about 100 maxims. In a way the maxims in the form we collected and arranged topically was an achievement of sorts. It was raw data which needed lot more work to be done.

It is then that I started to cross check the maxims from authentic sources. I was introduced to the existence of V. S. Sukthankar's authentic Sanskrit Mahabharat by Ms. Preeti Verma, Assistant Professor in Sanskrit, BHU. She suggested that my work needs to be cross checked and verified from the said publication. I had the good fortune of being able to locate the complete work of VS Sukthankar's Mahabharata on internet. It is then that Dr. Shashi Prabhu Kumar, a renowned Sanskrit Scholar of great eminence, suggested that I refer to K.M.Ganguli's English translation of Mahabharata which is considered an authoritative translation from Sanskrit.

I started cross checking the work with Sanskrit version in Sukthankar's publications and confirming the gist/ bhavartha which I was giving to each maxim from English Mahabharata by K.M. Ganguli. At this stage I was introduced to Ms. Sanhita Jani Vyas, a young and energetic Sanskrit Teacher based in Pune. She offered to compose the verses which we had compiled into the document. She contributed with her enthusiasm and also kept prodding me to complete the work when I started to lag. The Sanskrit verses were then run through some tools available on internet for getting the transliteration. Vishnu, was very enthusiastic and used his skills in this process to a great extent and helped me focus on other details.

Once we had the Sanskrit verse, English Transliteration and Gist in English I thought the task was complete. At that stage I had shared some part of the work with Sri K. Parasaran, who was in Chennai for his guidance. He very kindly had gone through the same and suggested that it is important to identify who is saying the particular verse which we had compiled. For Devil can also recite verses to suit its purpose. Realising that it was important to trace the name of the character I had to go through the entire work again literally 'verse by verse'. At this stage a well wisher and friend Sri Dalip Singh, a senior journalist, whom I requested to share his thoughts and give feedback on the work, suggested that if a primer could be added then the Maxims will become more meaningful. Another critical feedback which was quite a bitter pill indeed as it sent me back to a more laborious research to give the context for each Maxim. This task needed lot more time to narrate the story and the context of the maxims. I can say this was the most difficult task.

The contexts and gist may be embellished due to my limitations and I do not claim it to be the only possible understanding. However, I did make all efforts bonafide to make it as relateable to contemporary readers as possible.

The Book is meant for all, as eternal values for life have to be inculcated and nurtured all through the life by everyone irrespective of their identities or moorings for harmonious living of all species.

Chapter 1

Dharma

CONTEXT:

On being invited for a game of dice by Ḍhritaraśtra, the Pāṇḍava's come to Hastināpura. As part of the evil design, Duryodhana's maternal uncle, plays with Yudhiṣṭhira on behalf of Duryodhana and deceitfully defeats Yudhiṣṭhira and encourages him to wager more. During the course of the game, the Pāṇḍava's lose their entire wealth including their kingdom. Yudhiṣṭhira continues to gamble and loses his brothers, loses himself and on being prompted by Śakuni he even stakes Draupadī only to lose her.

Duryodhana commands his servant to go and fetch Draupadī to the assembly. The servant approaches Draupadī in her chambers and informs her about the game of dice where she was offered as stake and lost by Yudhiṣṭhira. On hearing this Draupadī raises the question whether Yudhiṣṭhira lost his freedom first or lost Draupadī first. The messenger presents the question posed by Draupadī in front of the assembly. Duryodhana commands his younger brother, Duḥśāsana, to go and fetch Draupadī and tell her that she will get her answer in the assembly in person. Draupadī declines to come to assembly as she was having her menstrual cycle and cannot present herself in that state in front of elders and the assembly. However, Duḥśāsana drags Draupadī by her hair to the assembly and attempts to disrobe her. The entire assembly watches silently in shock and does not react. Finding no savior in the Kuru assembly Draupadī prays to Lord Kṛṣṇa who through his illusion protects her modesty by supplying unending reams of robes. Duḥśāsana unable to disrobe her collapses due to fatigue.

Draupadī, seeks answer to her question from those present in the Kuru assembly, as to the legitimacy of her being offered as a wager by Yudhiṣṭhira when he already lost his freedom.

Prince Vikarṇa, a younger brother of Duryodhana, answers that Draupadī was not won in accordance with rules of Dharma. Prince Vikarṇa supports his argument by stating that Yudhiṣṭhira had lost himself before staking Draupadī and being a slave, himself could not stake Draupadī. Further, he points out that the rules of gambling prohibit an opponent from suggesting the wager to another player.

Vidura then chides the silent Kuru Assembly and reminds them of the duty of the Assembly to provide redress to a person who seeks justice. He narrates an anecdote wherein King Prahlāda was required to decide on a dispute involving his son Virocana and Sudhanvan, a Brāhmaṇa, as to who was superior between the two. In support of their claim of superiority they staked their respective life in wager to the winner.

King Prahlāda was hesitant as he was required to adjudicate a dispute involving the life of his own son and approaches Ṛṣi Kaśyapa for guidance. Ṛṣi Kaśyapa reminds the King that the dharma of the Assembly is to adjudicate the grievance brought before it by a person who comes seeking redressal from the injury. When a person suffering injustice approaches the Assembly seeking redressal, all those present are duty bound to provide redressal by rendering justice. Otherwise, those members of the assembly who were present in the assembly but fail to provide redressal shall partake the sin of such injustice.

विद्धो धर्मो ह्यधर्मेन सभां यत्र प्रपद्यते।
न चास्य शल्यं कृन्तन्ति विद्धास्तत्र सभासदः॥

viddho dharmo hyadharmena sabhāṃ yatra prapadyate|
na cāsya śalyaṃ kṛntanti viddhāstatra sabhāsadaḥ||

Dharma, when pierced by a dart of in justice, seeks redress in an Assembly, it is the duty of everyone in such assembly to take out the dart, else they themselves will incur the sin in failing to perform their duty.

Ṛṣikaśyapa, Sabhā Parva Ch.61 V.69

CONTEXT:

Bhīṣma, hearing Vidura's taunting the silence of the elders in the Kuru Assembly to the question of Draupadī, replies as follows. In this verse he states a universal truth of how the words of those in power are considered proper though it may not be so.

बलवांस्तु यथा धर्मं लोके पश्यति पूरुषः।
स धर्मो धर्मवेलायां भवत्यभिहितः परैः॥

balavāṃstu yathā dharmaṃ loke paśyati pūruṣaḥ|
sa dharmo dharmavelāyāṃ bhavatyabhihitaḥ paraiḥ||

Dharma is regarded by society, as that which a powerful man says it is, though it may be otherwise in reality. However, that which a weak man calls Dharma is rarely regarded as such even though it may be the highest Dharma.

Bhīṣma, Sabhā Parva Ch.62 V.15

CONTEXT:

Pāṇḍava's, after being defeated in the game of dice, leave for forest as agreed to spend twelve years in forest and 1 year incognito. Draupadī during their exile questions Yudhiṣṭhira on why he chooses to follow a path which is different from his forefathers and actively not seeking to regain the Kingdom, but instead has chosen to suffer in forest. Draupadī recalls how Yudhiṣṭhira is devoted towards Dharma, and exercised sovereignty for upholding Dharma alone. He would abandon Bhīma, Arjuna, Nakula and Sahadeva and even her for the sake of Dharma. Draupadī recalls hearing, that Dharma protects the king who protects Dharma and wonders why Dharma has not protected Yudhiṣṭhira.

राजानं धर्मगोप्तारं धर्मो रक्षति रक्षितः ॥

rājānaṃ dharmagoptāraṃ dharmo rakṣati rakṣitaḥ||

King protects Dharma and Dharma protects those who protect it.

Draupadī, Vana Parva Ch.31 V.07

CONTEXT:

The Pāṇḍava's on completing the period of 12 years in forest and one year incognito as per the condition of wager in the game of dice consult with their well-wishers on future course of action. After hearing about this, Ḍhritaraśtra sends his trusted emissary Sanjaya to the Pāṇḍava's with an advice not to take any hasty steps. Sanjaya returns to Hastināpura and meets Ḍhritaraśtra and chides him for his blind love for his son and takes leave of the King stating the message of King Yudhiṣṭhira will be delivered in the Assembly. Ḍhritaraśtra becomes restless wondering what the message could be Sanjaya did not disclose in private. He calls his Counsel Vidura and informs that he is suffering from sleeplessness and requests Vidura to speak to him as to what would be conducive for a man who is suffering from sleeplessness. Vidura then gives a discourse which is popularly known as Vidura Nīti (Vidura's moral prescriptions). Vidura, reminds the King about his advice, at the time of birth of Duryodhana that he would cause destruction of the race and that he should be abandoned. In reply Ḍhritaraśtra agrees with what Vidura has said but says he is unable to abandon his son, while recalling the well known – Maxim, that where there is righteousness there is victory.

यतो धर्मस्ततो जयः।

Yato dharmastato jayaḥ|

Where Dharma is Victory is there

King Ḍhritaraśtra, UdyogaParva Ch.39 V.07

CONTEXT:

Despite all the attempts made by Pāṇḍava and ŚrīKṛṣṇa to bring peace between Pāṇḍava and Kauravas, Duryodhana refuses to return their kingdom, rejecting the compromise of even giving 5 villages to Pāṇḍava's as suggested by Śrī Kṛṣṇa. Hence, battle becomes imminent between the two. As both armies reach Kurukshethra and are battle ready, Yudhisthra seeing the vast army of Kauravas is anxious and asks Arjuna how they would be able to overcome the army led by Bhīṣma. Arjuna in reply recalls what Bhīṣma had himself said to Indra regarding victory in a battle and quotes the following verse.

न तथा बलवीर्याभ्यां विजयन्ते जिगीषवः।
यथा सत्यानृशं साभ्यां धर्मेणैवोद्यमेन च॥

na tathā balavīryābhyāṃ vijayante jigīṣavaḥ|
yathā satyānṛśaṃ sābhyāṃ dharmeṇaivodyamena ca||

They that are desirous of victory do not conquer by might and valour so much as by truth, compassion, effort and energy.

Arjuna, BhīṣmaParva Ch.21 V.10

CONTEXT:

Bhīṣma while lying on the bed of arrows instructs Yudhiṣṭhira on various branches of learning. The instructions are in the form of questions and answers with anecdotal references to events in the past. Yudhiṣṭhira asks Bhīṣma as to which Yajña has been ordained for the sake virtue and not for the acquisition of either heaven or wealth. Bhīṣma recalls the anecdote narrated to him by Nārada, wherein a Brāhmaṇa declines to sacrifice a deer in a Yajña, though tempted with heaven as a fruit of such sacrifice. Dharma who had come in the form of a deer, appreciates his conduct, and declares that the sacrifice of living creatures is not in conformity with dharma.

अहिंसा सकलो धर्मो॥

ahiṃsā sakalo dharmo||

Non-violence is a Universal Dharma.

Bhīṣma, ŚāntiParva, Ch.264 V.19

CONTEXT:

Bhīṣma while lying on the bed of arrows instructs Yudhiṣṭhira on various branches of learning. The instructions are in the form of questions and answers with anecdotal references to events in the past. Yudhiṣṭhira asks Bhīṣma, how does one achieve Dharma, Detachment and Moksha. In response Bhīṣma states that one who sets out to acquire wealth should do so by righteous means. By pursuing only such activities in which he sees merit. By doing so one gets friends, wealth and children and obtains happiness both during life and thereafter. Such person can master the desires arising from Sound, Touch, Taste, Form and Scent. Not being contended, he pursues detachment with an eye on knowledge. Realizing the impermanence of all the worlds he even gives up the fruits of virtue, including heaven, and only then one can obtain Moksha.

प्रज्ञा धर्मे च रमते धर्मञ्चैवोपजीवति।
सोऽथ धर्मादवाप्तेषुधनेषु कुरुते मनः॥

prajñā dharme ca ramate dharmaṃcaivopajīvati|
so'tha dharmādavāpteṣudhaneṣu kurute manaḥ||

A man, who seeks prosperity, seeks prosperity only by means approved by Dharma.

Bhīṣma, Śānti Parva, Ch.265 V.14, 15

तस्यैवसिञ्चतेमूलङ्गुणान्पश्यतियत्रवै॥

tasyaivasiñcatemūlaṃguṇānpaśyatiyatravai||

A pious man waters the roots of only those in which he sees merit, i.e., Dharma.

Bhīṣma, Śānti Parva, Ch.265 V.15

CONTEXT:

Bhīṣma while lying on the bed of arrows instructs Yudhiṣṭhira on various branches of learning. The instructions are in the form of questions and answers with anecdotal references to events in the past to make it easy to understand. Yudhiṣṭhira seeks to know about the features of Dharma.

मर्यादायां स्थितो धर्मः शमः शौचस्य लक्षणम्॥

maryādāyāṃ sthito dharmaḥ śamaḥ śaucasya lakṣaṇam||

Dharma is living within one's limits, it is manifested in self-restraint and purity.

Bhīṣma, Anuśāsana Parva Ch.23 V.25

CONTEXT:

Bhīṣma while lying on the bed of arrows instructs Yudhiṣṭhira on various branches of learning. The instructions are in the form of questions and answers with anecdotal references to events in the past. Yudhiṣṭhira seeks to understand how to decipher Dharma from amongst the three distinct Sources viz, the Vedas, Direct perception and Customs, since they appear to be at variance in some instances. Bhīṣma subtly chides Yudhiṣṭhira for this confusion and directs him to follow his instructions like a blind man or a person without sense would depend upon another. Bhīṣma then instructs that Dharma is only one and is indivisible, though it may be perceived from three different perspectives, i.e., from the interpretation of Vedas, what one feels to be just through his own perception or based on the customs and usage. Any conclusion based on any one of the three sources shall lead to only one Dharma. Any interpretation or inference or customs which does not confirm with Dharma, with its various attributes, shall be considered as not being correct.

एक एवेति जानीहि त्रिधा तस्य प्रदर्शनम्।
पृथक्त्वे चैव मे बुद्धिस्त्रयाणामपि वै तथा॥

eka eveti jānīhi tridhā tasya pradarśanam|
pṛthaktve caiva me buddhistrayāṇāmapi vai tathā||

Though being One and indivisible, dharma is perceived to be threefold as seen from the perspectives of scriptures, direct perception, and customary usage. The paths of these three, that constitute the foundation of Dharma, are distinctly laid down.

Bhīṣma, Anuśāsana Parva Ch.147 V.19

अहिंसा सत्यमक्रोधो दानमेतच्चतुष्टयम्।
अजातशत्रो सेवस्व धर्म एष सनातनः॥

ahiṃsā satyamakrodho dānametaccatuṣṭayam|
ajātaśatro sevasva dharma eṣa sanātanaḥ||

Non-violence, Truth, absence of Anger and Charity, for these four qualities constitute eternal Dharma.

Bhīṣma, Anuśāsana Parva Ch.147 V.22

CONTEXT:

Bhīṣma has a boon to choose the time of his death. On being injured in the battle by Arjuna he rests on a bed of arrows. After the decimation of Kauravas in the battle, Bhīṣma teaches Yudhiṣṭhira various aspects of Life. Bhīṣma while lying on the bed of arrows for

58 days addresses ŚrīKṛṣṇa and seeks his permission to leave the body, while recalling having admonished Duryodhana and advised him to make peace by seeking refuge in ŚrīKṛṣṇa.

यतःकृष्णस्ततो धर्मो यतो धर्मस्ततो जयः॥

yataḥ kṛṣṇastato dharmo yato dharmastato jayaḥ||

Wherever Kṛṣṇa is, Dharma will be there, and where Dharma is Victory shall be there.

Bhīṣma, AnuśāsanaParva Ch.153 V.39

Chapter 2

Truth

CONTEXT:

The Pāṇḍava's on completing the period of 12 years in forest and one year incognito, as per the condition of wager in the game of dice, consult with their well-wishers on their future course of action. After hearing about this Ḍhritaraśtra sends his trusted emissary Sanjaya to the Pāṇḍava with an advice not to take any hasty steps. Sanjaya returns to Hastināpura and meets Ḍhritaraśtra and chides him for his blind love for his son and takes leave of the King stating the message of King Yudhisthra shall be delivered next day in the Kuru Assembly. Ḍhritaraśtra becomes restless and unable to sleep wondering what the message could be carried by Sanjaya which he did not disclose in private. Having become sleepless and burning from inside he calls his advisor Counsel Vidura and informs him that he is experiencing about his sleeplessness and requests Vidura to speak to him about things which would be conducive for a man who is suffering from sleeplessness and is burning from inside. And so that it would enlighten his mind and reduce his anxiety. Vidura then gives a discourse which is popularly known as Vidura Nīti (Vidura's moral prescriptions). He begins the discourse by saying that be it pleasant or unpleasant one should speak truth to the one whose defeat he does not wish.

शुभं वा यदि वा पापं द्वेष्यं वा यदि वा प्रियम्।
अपृष्टस्तस्यतद्ब्रूयाद्यस्यनेच्छेत्पराभवम्॥

śubhaṃ vā yadi vā pāpaṃ dveṣyaṃ vā yadi vā priyam|
apṛṣṭastasyatadbrūyādyasyanecchetparābhavam||

Auspicious or inauspicious, liked or disliked, one should speak the truth to him whose defeat one does not wish, even though not solicited.

Vidura, Udyoga Parva Ch.34 V.04

सत्येन रक्ष्यते धर्मो विद्या योगेन रक्ष्यते।

Satyena rakṣyate dharmo vidyā yogena rakṣyate|

Truth protects Dharma, Knowledge is preserved by practice.

Vidura, Udyoga Parva Ch.34 V.37

CONTEXT:

Karṇa having taken over as the Commander of the Kuru Army unleashes death on the Pandava army. He defeats Yudhiṣṭhira and severely injures him, but leaves him alive to keep the word he had given to Kunti. Arjuna meanwhile hears about Yudhiṣṭhira's defeat in the hands of Karṇa and becomes anxious about his brother's wellbeing and requests Kṛṣṇa, his charioteer to turn the Chariot towards their camp to see Yudhiṣṭhira. As Arjuna enters the camp, Yudhiṣṭhira assumes that Karṇa is vanquished by Arjuna and praises him. However, on hearing that Karṇa was alive, Yudhiṣṭhira condemns Arjuna's valour and chides him to hand over his bow, 'Gāṇḍīva' to some other deserving warrior who may put it to better use. Arjuna immediately draws out his sword and seeing this Kṛṣṇa asks him, whom he wishes to vanquish. Arjuna informs Kṛṣṇa of his vow to kill anyone who taunts him to give away 'Gāṇḍīva' and to be truthful to his vow he shall behead Yudhiṣṭhira. Kṛṣṇa on hearing about this vow of

Arjuna expresses his doubt if Arjuna has learnt anything about Dharma or Truth.

Kṛṣṇa explains that truth as practiced is exceedingly difficult to be understood as regards to its essential attributes. Herein ŚriKṛṣṇa illustrates various situations of life where truth may not be spoken without any fear of incurring sin.

भवेत्सत्यमवक्तव्यं वक्तव्यमनृतं भवेत्।
सर्वस्वस्यापहारे तु वक्तव्यमनृतं भवेत्॥

Bhavet satyamavaktavyaṃ vaktavyamanṛtaṃ bhavet|
sarvasvasyāpahāre tu vaktavyamanṛtaṃ bhavet||

Truth may not be spoken, and untruth spoken where untruth would pose as truth and truth as untruth.

ŚriKṛṣṇa, Karṇa Parva Ch.49 V.28

प्राणात्यये विवाहे च वक्तव्यमनृतंभवेत्।
यत्रानृतं भवेत्सत्यं सत्यं चाप्यनृतं भवेत्॥

prāṇātyaye vivāhe ca vaktavyamanṛtaṃbhavet|
yatrānṛtaṃ bhavetsatyaṃ satyaṃ cāpyanṛtaṃ bhavet||

In times of peril to life and in marriage, falsehood becomes utterable.

ŚriKṛṣṇa, Karṇa Parva Ch.49 V.29

तादृशं पश्यते बालो यस्य सत्यमनुष्ठितम्।
सत्यानृतेविनिश्चित्य ततो भवति धर्मवित्॥

tādṛśaṃ paśyate bālo yasya satyamanuṣṭhitam|
satyānṛteviniścitya tato bhavati dharmavit||

One who practices the Truth, without knowing the difference between truth and falsehood is ignorant. One is said to be conversant with dharma only when one can distinguish between truth and falsehood.

ŚriKṛṣṇa, Karṇa Parva Ch.49 V.30

CONTEXT:

Bhīṣma while lying on the bed of arrows instructs Yudhiṣṭhira on various branches of learning. The instructions are in the form of questions and answers with anecdotal references to events in the past. Yudhiṣṭhira while speaking of truth being kept on a high altar by learned Men and Gods, asks Bhīṣma what the facets of 'truth' are. Bhīṣma lists out the facets which embody 'truth' as the highest Dharma.

सत्यं च समता चैव दमश्चैव न संशयः।
अमात्सर्यं क्षमा चैव ह्रीस्तितिक्षानसूयता॥
त्यागो ध्यानमथार्यत्वं धृतिश्च सततं स्थिरा।
अहिंसा चैव राजेन्द्र सत्याकारास्त्रयोदश॥

satyaṃ ca samatā caivadamaścaiva na saṃśayaḥ|
amātsaryaṃ kṣamā caiva hrīstitikṣānasūyatā||
tyāgo dhyānamathāryatvaṃ dhṛtiśca satataṃ sthirā|
ahiṃsā caiva rājendra satyākārāstrayodaśa||

The forms that Truth assumes are Impartiality, Self-control, Forgiveness, Modesty, Endurance, Goodness, Renunciation, Contemplation, Dignity, Fortitude, Compassion, and Abstention from injury. These, O great monarch, are the thirteen forms of Truth. Truth is immutable, eternal, and unchangeable.

Bhīṣma, Śānti Parva, Ch.156 V.8, 9

CONTEXT:

Bhīṣma while lying on the bed of arrows instructs Yudhiṣṭhira on various branches of learning. The instructions are in the form of questions and answers with anecdotal references to events in the past. In this instance he narrates the conversation between King Ikshvaku and a Brāhmaṇa, who dedicated himself to recitation of Vedas. The Brāhmaṇa offers the fruits of the said recitation of Vedas to the King, who seeks to know what those fruits are. Brāhmaṇa engaged in recitation of Vedas expresses his inability to state what those fruits of recitation of Vedas are. The King initially having agreed to accept fruits of recitation of vedas, Later declines to accept the same citing his duty as a King is only to 'Give' and that he cannot accept the gift. The Brāhmaṇa then lists the virtues of "truth" – while commending the king to stick to his word.

न यज्ञाध्ययने दानं नियमास्तारयन्ति हि।
तथा सत्यं परे लोके यथावै पुरुषर्षभ॥

na yajñādhyayane dānaṃ niyamāstārayanti hi|
tathā satyaṃ pare loke yathā vai puruṣarṣabha||

Neither religious rites, gifts, or penances can redeem either in this world or the other world like Truth.

Bhīṣma, Śānti Parva Ch.192 V.61

तुलामारोपितो धर्मः सत्यं चैवेति नः श्रुतम्।
समां कक्षां धारयतोयतः सत्यं ततोऽधिकम्॥

tulāmāropito dharmaḥ satyaṃ caiveti naḥ śrutam|
samāṃ kakṣāṃ dhārayatoyataḥsatyaṃ tato'dhikam||

Truth and religious observances when weighed on a scale, Truth was seen to be heavier.

Bhīṣma, Śānti Parva Ch.192 V.68

यतो धर्मस्ततः सत्यं सर्वं सत्येन वर्धते॥

Yato dharma statah satyaṃ sarvaṃ satyena vardhate||

Wherever Dharma prevails truth is there, everything flourishes with Truth.

Bhīṣma, Śānti Parva Ch.192 V.69

CONTEXT:

Yudhiṣṭhira inquiries about the fruits attached to various good practices. Bhīṣma spells out various fruits attached to good practices and highlights the superior status of Truth amongst all such good practices.

धारणं सर्व वेदानां सर्वतीर्थावगाहनम्।
सत्यं च ब्रुवतो नित्यं समं वा स्यान्न वा समम्॥

dhāraṇaṃ sarva vedānāṃ sarvatīrthāvagāhanam|
satyaṃ ca bruvatonityaṃsamaṃvāsyānnavāsamam||

Memorizing all scriptures or visiting all holy places, may or may not be equal to always speaking the truth.

Bhīṣma, Anuśāsana Parva Ch.74 V.28

सत्येन सूर्यस्तपति सत्येनाग्निः प्रदीप्यते।
सत्येन मारुतो वाति सर्वं सत्ये प्रतिष्ठितम्॥

satyena sūryastapati satyenāgniḥ pradīpyate|
satyena māruto vāti sarvaṃ satye pratiṣṭhitam||

It is by the truth that the sun is imparting heat, it is by truth that fire gives light, it is by the truth that the winds blow; certainly, everything rests upon truth.

Bhīṣma, Anuśāsana Parva Ch.74 V.30

CONTEXT:

Bhīṣma who was on the bed of arrows for 58 days finally addresses the Pāṇḍava headed by Ḍhritaraśtra and other friends and well-wishers and leaves his parting instruction that truth is the greatest power.

सत्यं हि परमं बलम्॥

satyaṃ hi paramaṃ balam||

Truth is the greatest strength.

Bhīṣma, Anuśāsana Parva Ch.153 V.47

CONTEXT:

Bhīṣma while lying on the bed of arrows instructs Yudhiṣṭhira on various branches of learning. The instructions are in the form of questions and answers with anecdotal references to events in the past. In this instance Bhīṣma narrates the conversation between Goddess Umā with her spouse Lord Mahādeva. Goddess Umā asks Lord what makes a person enslaved and uttering what words one may be freed from one's bonds. In reply Lord Maheśvara speaks of qualities of wise men.

शुभः सत्यगुणो नित्यं वर्जनीया मृषा बुधैः॥

śubhaḥ satyaguṇo nityaṃ varjanīyā mṛṣā budhaiḥ||

Wise men always avoid untruth.

Lord Maheswara, Anuśāsana Parva Ch.132 V.26

Chapter 3

Principles Governing Punishment

CONTEXT:

Pursuant to their exile after losing game of dice with Kauravas, Pāṇḍava enter the forest and start living there. Draupadī provokes Yudhiṣṭhira with her words and exhorts him to give up his nature to be forgiving. She questions him as to why he does not get angry remembering all the wrongs done to them by Kauravas, forcing them to live in forests far from the comforts of their Palace despite the valour of Bhīma, Arjuna, Nakula and Sahadeva.

Draupadī cites the conversation between King Prahlāda with his grandson Bali where he instructs as to how punishment has to be administered having regard to the intention of the accused and circumstances in which the offence was committed.

पूर्वोपकारी यस्तुस्यादपराधोऽगरीयसि।
उपकारेण तत्तस्य क्षन्तव्यमपराधिनः॥

Pūrvopakārī yastusyādaparādho'garīyasi|
upakāreṇa tattasya kṣantavyamaparādhinaḥ||

One who has done a favor in the past, even though may be guilty of a grave wrong done to you, should be forgiven remembering the past favour.

King Prahlada Vana Parva Ch.29 V.25

अबुद्धिमाश्रितानां च क्षन्तव्यमपराधिनाम्।
न हि सर्वत्र पाण्डित्यं सुलभं पुरुषेणवै॥

abuddhimāśritānāṃ ca kṣantavyamaparādhinām|
na hi sarvatra pāṇḍityaṃ sulabhaṃ puruṣeṇavai||

One who commits an offence due to ignorance or foolishness deserves to be forgiven for learning and wisdom are not always easily attainable by man.

King Prahlada Vana Parva Ch.29 V.26

अथचेद्बुद्धिजं कृत्वा ब्रूयुस्तेतदबुद्धिजम्।
पापान्स्वल्पेऽपितान्हन्यादपराधे तथानृजून्॥

athacedbuddhijaṃ kṛtvā brūyustetadabuddhijam|
pāpānsvalpe'pitānhanyādaparādhe tathānṛjūn||

Those who knowingly commit an offence and plead ignorance should be punished even if the offence is minor.

King Prahlada, Vana Parva Ch.29 V.27

सर्वस्यैकोऽपराधस्ते क्षन्तव्यःप्राणिनोभवेत्।
द्वितीये सति वध्यस्तुस्वल्पेऽप्यपकृते भवेत्॥

sarvasyaiko'parādhaste kṣantavyaḥ prāṇino bhavet|
dvitīye sati vadhyastusvalpe'pyapakṛte bhavet||

Everyone deserves to be forgiven for the first offence, however second offence even trivial should be punished.

King Prahlada Vana Parva Ch.29 V.28

अजानता भवेत्कश्चिदपराधः कृतोयदि।
क्षन्तव्यमेवतस्याहुः सुपरीक्ष्य परीक्षया॥

Ajānatā bhavetkaścidaparādhaḥ kṛtoyadi|
kṣantavyamevatasyāhuḥ suparīkṣya parīkṣayā||

When a person commits an offence unknowingly, after due verification of his explanation he shall be forgiven.

King Prahlada, Vana Parva Ch.29 V.29

CONTEXT:

Yudhiṣṭhira after the epic battle sinks into grief for the great carnage leading to the demise of his friends and relatives. Seeing him overcome by grief his mother Kunti, wife Draupadī, and brothers Bhīma, Arjuna, Nakula, and Sahadeva remind him the duties of a King, as ordained. It is in this context that Arjuna recalls to Yudhiṣṭhira the necessity of punishment for maintaining order in the society.

यस्माददान्तान्दमयत्य शिष्टान्दण्डयत्यपि।
दमनाद्दण्डनाच्चैव तस्माद्दण्डं विदुर्बुधाः॥

Yasmādadāntāndamayatya śiṣṭāndaṇḍayatyapi|
damanāddaṇḍanāccaiva tasmāddaṇḍaṃ vidurbudhāḥ||

The wise have recognized punishment as a device to govern the unruly and punish the deviants.

Arjuna, Śānti Parva, Ch.15 V.8

अन्धंतम इवेदं स्यान्नप्रज्ञायेत किञ्चन।
दण्डश्चेन्नभवेल्लोके विभजन्साध्व साधुनी॥

andhaṃtama ivedaṃ syānnaprajñāyeta kiñcana|
daṇḍaścennabhavelloke vibhajansādhva sādhunī||

Darkness and destitution will prevail and people will fight, but for the fear of punishment.

Arjuna, Śānti Parva, Ch.15 V.32

सर्वो दण्डजितो लोके दुर्लभोहि शुनिश्चरः।
दण्डस्य हि भयाद्भीतो भोगयेह प्रकल्पते॥

Sarvo daṇḍajito loke durlabhohi śuniścaraḥ|
daṇḍasya hi bhayādbhīto bhogayeha prakalpate||

Everyone follows rules for fear of punishment, except for a few good persons. Fear of punishment is what makes people abide by rules.

Arjuna, Śānti Parva, Ch.15 V.34

विश्वलोपः प्रवर्तेत भिद्येरन्सर्व सेतवः।
ममत्वं न प्रजानीयुर्यदि दण्डो न पालयेत्॥

viśvalopaḥ pravarteta bhidyeransarva setavaḥ|
mamatvaṃ na prajānīyuryadi daṇḍo na pālayet||

Destruction and Confusion shall prevail everywhere, the concept of ownership lost but for fear of punishment.

Arjuna, Śānti Parva, Ch.15 V.38

चरेयुर्नाश्रमेधर्मं यथोक्तं विधिमाश्रिताः।
नविद्यां प्राप्नुयात्कश्चिद्यदि दण्डो न पालयेत्॥

careyurnāśramedharmaṃ yathoktaṃ vidhimāśritāḥ|
navidyāṃ prāpnuyātkaścidyadi daṇḍo na pālayet||

Everyone follows their respective Dharma and acquires knowledge, due to fear of punishment.

Arjuna, Śānti Parva, Ch.15 V.40

अर्थे सर्वे समारम्भाः समायत्ता न संशयः।
स च दण्डे समायत्तः पश्य दण्डस्य गौरवम्॥

Arthe sarve samārambhāḥ samāyattā na saṃśayaḥ|
sa ca daṇḍe samāyattaḥ paśya daṇḍasya gauravam||

Wealth makes possible all activities without any doubt, which in turn is possible due to fear of punishment.

Arjuna, Śānti Parva, Ch.15 V.48

दण्डः शास्तिप्रजाः सर्वादण्ड एवाभिरक्षति।
दण्डः सुप्तेषु जागर्ति दण्डं धर्मं विदुर्बुधाः॥

daṇḍaḥ śāstiprajāḥ sarvādaṇḍa evābhirakṣati|
daṇḍaḥ supteṣu jāgarti daṇḍaṃ dharmaṃ vidurbudhāḥ||

Power to punish controls people and in turn, protects them. Power to punish is awake when everyone else is asleep, hence is also equated with Dharma.

Arjuna, Śānti Parva, Ch.15 V.02

लोकयात्रार्थमेवेह धर्मप्रवचनं कृतम्।
अहिंसा साधुहिंसेति श्रेयान्धर्मपरिग्रहः॥

Lokayātrārthameveha dharmapravacanaṃ kṛtam|
ahiṃsā sādhuhiṃseti śreyāndharmaparigrahaḥ||

Duties have been ordained to people for maintaining the various relations of the world. Abstention from injuriy is good but that which holds dharma is preferable.

Arjuna, Śānti Parva Ch.15 V.49

Chapter 4

Karma

CONTEXT:

Queen Gāndhāri, mother of Duryodhana, on hearing about the humiliation of Draupadī in the Kuru Assembly and the deceitful acquisition of entire wealth and kingdom of Pāṇḍava in gambling by Kauravas, strongly reprimands her sons. She states that wealth acquired by cruel acts shall be destroyed, while wealth acquired by fair means shall last.

प्रध्वंसिनी क्रूरसमाहिता श्रीर्मृदुप्रौढा गच्छति पुत्रपौत्रान्॥

pradhvaṃsinī krūrasamāhitā
śrīrmṛduprauḍhā gacchati putrapautrān||

Prosperity acquired by cruel acts, is soon destroyed. Whereas, prosperity acquired by benign methods stays with children and grandchildren.

Queen Gāndhāri, Sabhā Parva Ch.66 V.35

CONTEXT:

ŚriKṛṣṇa in his eternal discourse popularly known as Bhagavadgīta spells out certain eternal truths. This discourse happens in the midst of two Armies ready to face each other in the battlefield of Kurukshetra. ŚriKṛṣṇa dispels the darkness which had taken over the mind of Arjuna and guides him out through the light of knowledge.

न हि कल्याण कृत्कश्चिद्दुर्गतिं तात गच्छति॥

na hi kalyāṇa kṛtkaściddurgatiṃ tata gacchati||

One who does good, does not reach a miserable end.

ŚriKṛṣṇa, Bhagavadīgtā, Bhīṣma Parva Ch.28 V.40

सत्त्वात्सञ्जायते ज्ञानं रजसो लोभ एव च।
प्रमाद मोहौ तमसो भवतोऽज्ञानमेव च॥

Sattvātsañjāyate jñānaṃ rajaso lobha eva ca|
pramāda mohua tamaso bhavato'jñānameva ca||

Sattva guṇa results in knowledge, Rajas in materialism and Tamas leads to error, delusion, and ignorance.

ŚriKṛṣṇa, Bhagavadīgtā, Bhīṣma Parva Ch.36 V.17

CONTEXT:

Yudhiṣṭhira after the epic battle sinks into grief for the great carnage leading to the destruction of the entire Kaurava clan. Seeing him overcome by grief his mother Kunti, wife Draupadī, and brothers Bhīma, Arjuna, Nakula, and Sahadeva remind him the duties of a King, as ordained. It is in this context that Arjuna reminds Yudhiṣṭhira that every "action" has some good and bad intrinsically in it.

नात्यन्तगुणवान्कश्चिन्न चाप्यत्यन्त निर्गुणः।
उभयं सर्वकार्येषु दृश्यते साध्व साधुच॥

nātyantaguṇavānkaścinna cāpyatyanta nirguṇaḥ|
ubhayaṃ sarvakāryeṣu dṛśyate sādhva sādhu ca||

There is no act which is entirely pure, nor any that is entirely simple; in every act right or wrong something of both prevails.

Arjuna, Śānti Parva Ch.15 V.50

CONTEXT:

Bhīṣma while lying on a bed of arrows instructs Yudhiṣṭhira on various branches of learning. The instructions are in the form of questions and answers with anecdotal references to events in the past. Yudhiṣṭhira inquires as to what follows the Ātmā to the other world after leaving the dead body. At that point Bhīṣma observes, Ṛṣi Bṛhaspati was approaching them and suggests that the query should be addressed to him. On hearing the query Ṛṣi Bṛhaspati says that every person comes to this world alone and goes alone from this world. That he suffers alone the difficulties one meets and alone encounters whatever misery falls to one's lot. It is only his Karma which follows him to the next world. Yudhiṣṭhira then asks as to how Karma follows even after death. Ṛṣi Bṛhaspati states that witnesses to one's conduct are eternal enabling karma to follow even after death. The core of Karma philosophy is premised on the belief of re-birth, which can be in any form of life depending on one's Karma, including that as a human. The consequences of good or bad karma would have to be experienced either during the same life or in a subsequent life.

पृथिवीवायुराकाशमापोज्योतिश्च पञ्चमम्।
बुधिरात्मा च सहिता धर्मं पश्यन्ति नित्यदा॥
प्राणिनामिह सर्वेषां साक्षिभूतानिचानिशम्।
एतैश्चसहधर्मोऽपितं जीवमनुगच्छति॥

pṛthivīvāyurākāśamāpojyotiśca pañcamam|
budhirātmā ca sahitā dharmaṃ paśyanti nityadā||
prāṇināmiha sarveṣāṃ sākṣibhūtānicāniśam|
etaiścasahadharmo'pitaṃ jīvamanugacchati||

Earth, Wind, Space, Water, Light, Mind, Yama, Understanding, Ātmāas also Day and Night all together are witnesses of the conduct of all living beings at all times. With these, Dharma follows the creatures after death.

Bṛhaspati, AnuśāsanaParva Ch.112 V.20,21

CONTEXT:

Bhīṣma while lying on the bed of arrows instructs Yudhiṣṭhira on various branches of learning. The instructions are in the form of questions and answers with anecdotal references to events in the past. Yudhiṣṭhira wonders between Destiny and Karma in the present, which is more powerful? Bhīṣma refers to the conversation between Lord Brahma and Sage Vasishta wherein, Lord Brahma clear the doubt of Sage Vasishta in this regard. Lord Brahma likens Destiny or Prārabdha Karma to a seed and Karma or exertion in the present to the soil. It is the union of these two that one has good or bad experiences in the current life. One can enhance or diminish what one is destined with through his Karma in the present. Lord Brahma therefore concludes that exertion in the present is more powerful.

आत्मैव ह्यात्मनो बन्धुरात्मैव रिपुरात्मनः।
आत्मैव चात्मनः साक्षी कृतस्याप्यकृतस्य च॥

ātmaiva hyātmano bandhurātmaiva ripurātmanaḥ|
ātmaiva cātmanaḥ sākṣī kṛtasyāpyakṛtasya ca||

Oneself, is his own friend as much as his own foe, as well as the witness of one's good and evil deeds.

Lord Brahma, Anuśāsana Parva Ch.06 V.27

न च फलति विकर्मा जीवलोकेन दैवम्॥
व्यपनयति विमार्गं नास्ति दैवे प्रभुत्वं, गुरुमिव कृतमग्र्यं कर्म संयाति दैवम्।
अनुपहतमदीनम्कामकारेण दैवं, नयति पुरुषकारः संचितस्तत्र तत्र॥

na ca phalati vikarmā jīvalokena daivam||
vyapanayati vimārgaṃ nāsti daive prabhutvaṃ, gurumiva kṛtamagryaṃ karma saṃyāti daivam|
anupahatamadīnam kāmakāreṇa daivaṃ, nayati puruṣakāraḥ saṃcitastatra tatra||

A person who does not engage in karma is never content in this world nor can Destiny alter the course of a man who has strayed. As the pupil follows one's preceptor, so does Destiny follow Exertion. The affairs in which one's own exertion is seen, there Destiny shows its hand.

Lord Brahma, Anuśāsana Parva, Ch.06 V.47

CONTEXT:

Bhīṣma while lying on a bed of arrows instructs Yudhiṣṭhira on various branches of learning. The instructions are in the form of questions and answers with anecdotal references to events in the past. Yudhiṣṭhira laments seeing his grandfather lying on a bed of arrows and seeks his guidance to cleanse his sins, Bhīṣma consoles him and narrates the anecdote of an Old Lady, Gautami, who loses her young son to a snake bite. Seeing her suffer in grief on the untimely death of her son a hunter named Arjunaka catches hold of the snake and seeks to avenge the death of her son by killing the snake. Gautami rebukes Arjunaka and states that the inevitable cannot be undone and there is no purpose in committing sin by seeking retribution. The conversation is very subtle on who is responsible for the untimely death of a young man the Snake or Death or Time or Karma. In the final analysis the real cause of untimely death of the young man is found to be due to his own karma. The interesting discourse brings out the essence of Karma philosophy, which can calm an agitated mind and provide solace.

यथा मृत्पिण्डतःव कर्ता कुरुतेयद्यदिच्छति।
एवमात्मकृतं कर्म मानवः प्रतिपद्यते॥

Yathā mṛtpiṇḍataḥ va kartā kurute yadyadicchati|
evamātmakṛtaṃ karma mānavaḥ pratipadyate||

As men make from a lump of clay whatever they wish to make, even so, do men attain varied results determined by their own Karma.

Kāla (Time), Anuśāsana Parva Ch.1 V.67

Chapter 5

Hygiene as Good Conduct

CONTEXT:

Bhīṣma while lying on the bed of arrows instructs Yudhiṣṭhira on various branches of learning. The instructions are in the form of questions and answers. Bhīṣma spells out the traits of good and bad persons. A person who follows sanitary hygiene was considered as being of good conduct.

पुरीषं यदि वामूत्रं ये न कुर्वन्तिमानवाः।
राजमार्गे गवां मध्ये धान्यमध्ये च तेशुभाः॥

purīṣaṃ yadi vāmūtraṃ ye na kurvantimānavāḥ|
rājamār gegavāṃ madhye dhānyamadhye ca teśubhāḥ||

The good or the righteous never answer the calls of nature on the public road, in Cowpens or the paddy field.

Bhīṣma, Śānti Parva Ch.186 V.03

राजमार्गे गवां मध्ये गोष्ठमध्ये च धर्मिणः।
नोपसेवन्ति राजेन्द्र सर्गं मूत्रपुरीषयोः॥

Rājamārge gavāṃ madhye goṣṭhamadhye ca dharmiṇaḥ|
nopasevanti rājendra sargaṃ mūtrapurīṣayoḥ||

The righteous men never answer the calls of nature on a public road, or in the midst of a cow-pen, or in a field of paddy.

Bhīṣma, Anuśāsana Parva Ch.148 V.09

Chapter 6

Nature

CONTEXT:

Vidura speaks of state craft, morality and ethics to Ḍhritaraśtra, in his discourse popularly known as ViduraNīti. Vidura tries to use similes to convince Ḍhritaraśtra that Pāṇḍava and Kauravas are interdependent and cannot be defeated when they are together. Vidura advises Ḍhritaraśtra on what actions he should take in view of the imminent hostility between Kauravas and Pāṇḍava. He compares Kauravas to creepers and the Pāṇḍava as the trees on which the creepers can grow. Vidura then compares the Kauravas to a forest and Pāṇḍava to the tigers, in an attempt to dissuade Ḍhritaraśtra from allowing Duryodhana prevail in forcing a battle with Pāṇḍava.

सिंहैर्विहीनं हि वनं विनश्येत्सिंहाविनश्येयुर्ऋते वनेन॥

siṃhairvihīnaṃ hi vanaṃ vinaśyetsiṃhāvinaśyeyurṛte vanena||

A forest without lions is destroyed and lions without forest will perish.

Vidura, Udyoga Parva Ch.37 V.60

नस्याद्वनमृते व्याघ्रान्व्याघ्रानस्युर्ऋते वनम्।
वनं हि रक्ष्यते व्याघ्रैर्व्याघ्रात्रक्षति काननम्॥

nasyādvanamṛte vyāghrānvyāghrānasyurṛte vanam|
vanaṃ hi rakṣyate vyāghrairvyāghrānrakṣati kānanam||

Tigers without forest and forest without tigers cannot exist. Forest protects tigers and the tigers protect the forest.

Vidura, Udyoga Parva Ch.37 V.42

CONTEXT:

Ḍhritaraśtra requests Sanjaya to speak about the land of Bhāratavarśa, to gain control over which the huge armies of Kauravas and Pāṇḍava had assembled for battle in Kurukshetra. Sanjaya describes the geographical features of Bhārata Varsha and the great people who have inhabited in it and ruled over it. After describing in detail, the names of various mountains, rivers, Kingdoms, Sanjaya speaks of the great quality of Earth as a provider. One may recall what Mahātmā Gandhi stated, 'earth can provide for man's needs, not for his greed', something which may have been inspired from this verse.

यथा गुणबलं चापि त्रिवर्गस्य महाफलम्।
दुह्येद्धेनुः कामधुक्कभूमिः सम्यगनुष्ठिता॥

Yathā guṇabalaṃ cāpi trivargasya mahāphalam|
duhyeddhenu: kāmadhuvkabhūmi: samyaganuṣiṭhatā||

The three-fold fruits of Dharma, Wealth and Pleasures can be milked from the earth, like from a wish giving Cow, if the resources are used prudently.

Sanjaya, BhīṣmaParva Ch.10 V.69

पितामाताचपुत्रश्च खंद्यौश्चनरपुङ्गव।

Pitāmātācaputraśca khaṃdyauścanarapuṅgava|

If the earth is properly treated, it becomes father, mother, child and heaven for all creatures.

Sanjaya, BhīṣmaParva Ch.10 V.74

CONTEXT:

Bhīṣma while lying on a bed of arrows instructs Yudhiṣṭhira on various branches of learning. The instructions are in the form of questions and answers with anecdotal references to events. When asked about merits of gifts, Bhīṣma proceeds to refer to the conversation between Gods and Lord Brahma. In this conversation Lord Brahma while stating the benefits of making Gifts of Land states that religious ceremonies performed on land owned by others would be futile, however those performed in Holy places would be fruitful. Since there are no owners to natural resources and holy places.

अटवीपर्वताश्चैव नदीतीर्थानि यानि च।
सर्वाण्यस्वामिकान्याहुर्नहि तत्र परिग्रहः॥

aṭavīparvatāścaiva nadītīrthāni yāni ca|
sarvāṇyasvāmikānyāhurna hi tatra parigrahaḥ||

Forest, mountains, rivers and holy places are regarded as having no owners. Hence, for performing religious rituals, land need not be purchased.

Lord Brahma, Anuśāsana Parva Ch.65 V.34

Chapter 7

Faith

CONTEXT:

After the Pāṇḍava's leave for forest upon losing their kingdom in the game of dice, Ṛṣi Nārada appears in the Kuru Assembly and warns that after 13 years the Pāṇḍava will come back and claim their Kingdom by destroying the Kuru race. Upon hearing this Duryodhana, Duḥśāsana and Karṇa approach their Guru Droṇācārya and offer the entire kingdom to him seeking his protection. Droṇācārya assures them of his protection however says this,

दैवमूलमतःपरम्॥

daivamūlamataḥparam||

God's will shall prevail.

Dronacharya, Sabhā Parva Ch.71 V.35

CONTEXT:

The Pāṇḍava on completing the period of 12 years in forest and one year incognito, as per the condition of wager in the game of dice, consult with their well-wishers on their future course of action. After hearing about this Ḍhritaraśtra sends his trusted emissary Sanjaya to the Pāṇḍava with an advice not to take any hasty steps. Sanjaya returns to Hastināpura and meets Ḍhritaraśtra and chides him for his blind love for his son and takes leave of the King stating the message of King Yudhisthra shall be delivered next day in the Kuru Assembly. Ḍhritaraśtra becomes restless and unable to sleep wondering what the message could be carried by Sanjaya which he did not disclose in private. He calls his advisor Vidura and informs him that he is experiencing sleeplessness and requests Vidura to speak to him about things which would be conducive for a man who is suffering from sleeplessness and is burning from inside. So that it would enlighten his mind and reduce his anxiety. Vidura then gives a discourse which is popularly known as Vidura Nīti (Vidura's moral prescriptions).

पञ्चाग्नयोमनुष्येणपरिचर्याःप्रयत्नतः।
पितामाताग्निरात्मा च गुरुश्च भरतर्षभ॥

pañcāgnayomanuṣyeṇaparicaryāḥprayatnataḥ|
pitāmātāgnirātmā ca guruśca bharatarṣabha||

Five fires which are to be worshipped are Father, Mother, Ātmā, Fire and Guru.

Vidura, Udyoga Parva Ch.33 V.62

CONTEXT:

Yudhisthra on seeing the vast army of Kauravas is anxious and asks Arjuna how they would defeat the army led by Bhīṣma. Arjuna in reply recalls what Nārada had said regarding victory being an attribute of Kṛṣṇa and assures Yudhiṣṭhira that with Kṛṣṇa leading them they are bound to be victorious.

यतःकृष्णस्ततोजयः॥

yataḥkṛṣṇastatojayaḥ||

Wherever Kṛṣṇa is, victory shall be there.

Arjuna, Bhīṣma Parva Ch.21 V.12

CONTEXT:

ŚriKṛṣṇa in his discourse popularly known as Bhagavadgīta spells out certain eternal truths. This discourse happens in the midst of two Armies ready to face each other in the battlefield of Kurukshetra. ŚriKṛṣṇa dispels the darkness which had taken over the mind of Arjuna and guides him with the light of knowledge.

जातस्य हि ध्रुवो मृत्युर्ध्रुवं जन्ममृतस्य च।
तस्मादपरिहार्येऽर्थे न त्वं शोचितुमर्हसि॥

Jātasya hi dhruvo mṛtyurdhruvaṃ janmamṛtasya ca|
tasmādaparihāryesrthe na tvaṃ śocitumarhasi||

One that is born is bound to die, and one who dies is bound to be reborn. Grief for things which are certain is not warranted.

ŚriKṛṣṇa, Bhagavadgīta, BhīṣmaParva Ch.24 V.27

यदा यदा हि धर्मस्य ग्लानिर्भवति भारत।
अभ्युत्थानमधर्मस्य तदात्मानं सृजाम्यहम्॥

Yadā yadā hi dharmasya glānirbhavati bhārata|
abhyutthānamadharmasya tadātmānaṃ sṛjāmyaham||

Whenever, dharma languishes and evil flourishes I manifest myself.

ŚriKṛṣṇa, Bhagavadīgtā, Bhīṣma Parva Ch.26 V.07

परित्राणाय साधूनां विनाशाय च दुष्कृताम्।
धर्मसंस्थापनार्थाय संभवामि युगे युगे॥

paritrāṇāya sādhūnāṃ vināśāya ca duṣkṛtām|
dharmasaṃsthāpanārthāya saṃbhavāmi yuge yuge||

To protect the virtuous and destroy the wicked and for establishing Dharma I create myself in every era.

ŚriKṛṣṇa, Bhagavadīgtā, BhīṣmaParva Ch.26 V.08

सर्वभूतस्थितं यो मां भजत्येकत्वमास्थितः।
सर्वथा वर्तमानोऽपि सयोगीमयि वर्तते॥

sarvabhūtasthitaṃ yo māṃ bhajatyekatvamāsthitaḥ|
sarvathā vartamāno'pi sayogīmayi vartate||

One who sees the creator in all species, realising the Oneness, is a devotee who lives in God, whatever may be his mode of worldly life.

ŚriKṛṣṇa, Bhagavadīgtā, BhīṣmaParva Ch.28 V.31

आत्मौपम्येन सर्वत्र समं पश्यतियोऽर्जुन।
सुखं वा यदि वा दुःखं सयोगी परमोमतः॥

Ātmaupamyena sarvatra samaṃ paśyatiyo'rjuna|
sukhaṃ vā yadi vā duḥkhaṃ sayogī paramomataḥ||

One who sees equally all things as his own self, whether in pleasure or in pain, he is considered a perfect yogi.

ŚriKṛṣṇa, Bhagavadīgtā, Bhīṣma Parva Ch.28 V.32

यो यो यां यां तनुं भक्तःश्रद्धयार्चितुमिच्छति।
तस्य तस्याचलां श्रद्धां तामेवविदधाम्यहम्॥

Yo yo yāṃ yāṃ tanuṃ bhaktaḥ śraddhayārcitumicchati|
tasya tasyācalāṃ śraddhāṃ tāmevavidadhāmyaham||

Whatever be the form anyone worships with faith; I make that faith steady.

ŚriKṛṣṇa, Bhagavadīgtā, Bhīṣma Parva Ch.29 V.21

इदं शरीरं कौन्तेय क्षेत्रमित्यभिधीयते।
एतद्योवेत्ति तं प्राहुःक्षेत्रज्ञ इति तद्विदः॥

idaṃ śarīraṃ kaunteya kṣetramityabhidhīyate|
etadyovetti taṃ prāhuḥ kṣetrajña iti tadvidaḥ||

The human body is known as a field (kshetra), one who understands the difference between the body and himself, is known as the knower of the field (kshetrajna).

ŚriKṛṣṇa, Bhagavadīgtā, Bhīṣma Parva Ch.35 V.01

Chapter 8

Anger

CONTEXT:

Pursuant to their exile upon losing the game of dice with Kauravas, Pāṇḍava enter the forest and start living there. Draupadī provokes Yudhiṣṭhira with her words and exhorts him to give up his forgiving nature. She questions him as to why he does not get angry remembering all the wrongs done to them by Kauravas, forcing them to live in forests far from the comforts of their Palace despite the valour of Bhīma, Arjuna, Nakula and Sahadeva. Draupadī reminds him of the teaching of King Prahlāda to his grandson Bali on the relative demerits of forgiveness when compared to the use of might. King Prahlāda spells out the pros and cons of forgiveness as well as the use of might. Hearing Draupadī exhorting him to choose path of might befitting the Kshatriyas (the Warrior class), Yudhiṣṭhira replies highlighting the evil consequences of Anger.

यो हि संहरते क्रोधं भावस्तस्यसुशोभने।
यः पुनः पुरुषः क्रोधं नित्यं न सहते शुभे॥
तस्याभावाय भवति क्रोधः परमदारुणः॥

yo hi saṃharate krodhaṃ bhāvastasyasuśobhane|
yaḥ punaḥ puruṣaḥ krodhaṃ nityaṃ na sahate śubhe||
tasyābhāvāya bhavati krodhaḥ paramadāruṇaḥ||

One who conquers his anger prospers, whilst those who don't reap adversity as a consequence.

Yudhiṣṭhira, VanaParva Ch.30 V.02

क्रोधमूलो विनाशो हि प्रजानामिह दृश्यते।

krodhamūlo vināśo hi prajānāmi hadṛśyate|

Anger is the root cause of destruction of all creatures.

Yudhiṣṭhira, Vana Parva Ch.30 V.03

वाच्या वाच्ये हि कुपितो न प्रजानातिकर्हिचित्।
ना कार्यमस्तिक्रुद्धस्य नावाच्यं विद्यते तथा॥

vācyā vācye hi kupito na prajānātikarhicit|
nā kāryamastikruddhasya nāvācyaṃ vidyate tathā||

An angry person cannot distinguish between what should and should not be said. There is no act or word which an angry person may not do or say.

Yudhiṣṭhira, VanaParva Ch.30 V.05

हिंस्यात्क्रोधादवध्यांश्च वध्यान्सं पूजयेदपि।
आत्मानमपि च क्रुद्धःप्रेषयेद्यमसादनम्॥

hiṃsyātkrodhādavadhyāṃśca vadhyānsaṃ pūjayedapi|
ātmānamapi ca kruddhaḥ preṣayedyamasādanam||

Anger can make a man kill the one who does not deserve to be killed and adulate one who deserves to be killed. Anger can cause one's own death.

Yudhiṣṭhira, VanaParva Ch.30 V.06

मूढो यदि क्लिश्यमानःक्रुद्ध्यतेऽशक्तिमान्नरः।
बलीयसां मनुष्याणां त्यजत्यात्मानमन्ततः॥

mūḍho yadi kliśyamānaḥ kruddhyate'śaktimānnaraḥ|
balīyasāṃ manuṣyāṇāṃ tyajatyātmānamantataḥ||

A weak man when persecuted if foolishly becomes angry towards stronger men, causes his own destruction.

Yudhiṣṭhira, VanaParva Ch.30 V.10

दाक्ष्यं ह्यमर्षः शौर्यं च शीघ्रत्वमिति तेजसः।
गुणाः क्रोधाभिभूतेन न शक्याः प्राप्तुमञ्जसा॥

dākṣyaṃ hyamarṣaḥ śauryaṃ ca śīghratvamiti tejasaḥ|
guṇāḥ krodhābhibhūtena na śakyāḥ prāptumañjasā||

The man who is overwhelmed with wrath does not acquire with ease generosity, dignity, courage, skill, and other attributes of good character.

Yudhiṣṭhira, Vana Parva Ch.30 V.20

Chapter 9

Reputation

CONTEXT:

ŚriKṛṣṇa in his discourse popularly known as Bhagavadīgtā spells out certain eternal truths. This discourse happens in the midst of two Armies ready to face each other in the battlefield of Kurukshetra. ŚriKṛṣṇa dispels the darkness which had taken over the mind of Arjuna and guides him with the light of knowledge.

> संभावितस्यचाकीर्तिर्मरणादतिरिच्यते ॥
>
> saṃbhāvitasyacākīrtirmaraṇādatiricyate||
>
> A person who is held in respect, to him disrespect is worse than death itself.
>
> ŚriKṛṣṇa, Bhagavadīgtā, Bhīṣma Parva Ch.24 V.34

CONTEXT:

Karṇa having taken over as the Commander of the Kuru Army unleashes death on the Pandava army. He defeats Yudhiṣṭhira and severly injuries him, but leaves him alive to keep the word he had given to Kunti. Arjuna meanwhile hears about Yudhiṣṭhira's defeat in the hands of Karṇa and becomes anxious about his brother's well being and requests Kṛṣṇa, his charioteer to turn the Chariot towards their camp to see Yudhiṣṭhira. As Arjuna enters the camp,

Yudhiṣṭhira assumes that Karṇa is vanquished by Arjuna and praises him. However, on hearing that Karṇa was alive, Yudhiṣṭhira condemns Arjuna's valour and chides him to hand over his bow, 'Gāṇḍīva' to some other deserving warrior who may put it to better use. Arjuna immediately draws out his sword and seeing this Kṛṣṇa asks him, whom he wishes to vanquish. Arjuna informs Kṛṣṇa of his vow to kill anyone who taunts him to give 'Gāṇḍīva' and to be truthful to his vow he now shall behead Yudhiṣṭhira. Kṛṣṇa on hearing about this vow of Arjuna expresses his doubt if Arjuna has learnt anything about Dharma or Truth.

Kṛṣṇa having explained the circumstances when falsehood may be uttered without incurring sin suggests to Arjuna that death need not be necessarily caused by physical death of the person. Arjuna in order to keep his vow may address his older brother Yudhiṣṭhira disrespectfully instead of addressing him with respect as he does always. For being spoken to disrespectfully is as good as causing death to a person who is used to being respected.

यदावमानं लभते महान्तं, तदाजीवन्मृतइत्युच्यतेसः॥

yadāvamānaṃ labhate mahāntaṃ
tadājīvanmṛtaityucyatesaḥ||

A person who is always respected if he is disrespected, then he is as good as dead though alive.

ŚriKṛṣṇa, Karṇa Parva Ch.49 V.65

Chapter 10

Eternal Values

CONTEXT:

As Pāṇḍava's were leaving Hastināpura for forest on being exiled, the people of Hastināpura follow them and seek to stay in the company of Pāṇḍava's and avoid the company of Kauravas.

वस्त्रमापस्तिलान्भूमिं गन्धो वासयते यथा।
पुष्पाणामधिवासेन तथा संसर्गजा गुणाः॥

vastramāpastilānbhūmiṃ gandho vāsayate yathā|
puṣpāṇāmadhivāsena tathā saṃsargajā guṇāḥ||

Cloth, water, the ground, and sesame seeds acquire fragrance by their association with flowers, so are qualities acquired by association.

Citizen of Hastināpura, Vana Parva Ch.01 V.22

मोहजालस्य योनिर्हिमूढैरेव समागमः।
अहन्यहनिधर्मस्ययोनिः साधुसमागमः॥

mohajālasya yonirhimūḍhaireva samāgamaḥ|
ahanyahanidharmasyayoniḥ sādhusamāgamaḥ||

Delusion entangles the mind when associated with fools, while the association with the wise and the good leads one on the path of Dharma.

Citizen of Hastināpura, Vana Parva Ch.01 V.23

बुद्धिश्च हीयते पुंसां नीचैः सहसमागमात्।
मध्यमैर्मध्यतां याति श्रेष्ठतां यातिचोत्तमैः॥

Buddhiśca hīyate puṃsāṃ nīcaiḥ sahasamāgamāt|
madhyamairmadhyatāṃ yāti śreṣṭhatāṃ yāticottamaiḥ||

Association with those without scruples impairs the understanding, as indeed, with the indifferent makes one indifferent, while the association with the good exalts.

Citizen of Hastināpura, Vana Parva Ch.01 V.28

CONTEXT:

Unable to provide proper food and hospitality for the Brahmanas who were following Pāṇḍava's in forest, Yudhiṣṭhira is distressed and expresses his anguish to the Brahmaṇas apologetically requesting them to return to city. In reply Śaunaka, a Brahmana well versed in Knowledge of self and Sankhya system, addresses these soothing verses recalling that these verses were earlier chanted by King Janaka.

शोकस्थानसहस्त्राणिभयस्थानशतानि च।
दिवसेदिवसे मूढमाविशन्ति न पण्डितम्॥

śokasthānasahastrāṇibhayasthānaśatāni ca|
divasedivase mūḍhamāviśanti na paṇḍitam||

Grief in thousands and fear in hundreds day after day, overwhelm the ignorant but not the wise.

Śaunaka – a Brāhmaṇa, Vana Parva Ch.2 V.15

CONTEXT:

King Ḍhritaraśtra under the influence of his son Duryodhana orders the construction of a gaming Hall to invite the Pāṇḍava for a game of dice, a form of gambling. Vidura on coming to know of the decision of Ḍhritaraśtra cautions him of the evil that is going to visit them because of gambling. Ḍhritaraśtra on hearing Vidura's advice summons Duryodhana and advises him against his plan to invite Pāṇḍava for a game of dice to usurp their entire wealth. Duryodhana lists out the wealth and prosperity that he has witnessed during the RājasūyaYajña performed by the Pāṇḍava in Indraprastha thereby giving vent to his jealousy. Ḍhritarāśtra cautions his son Duryodhana of the evil consequences of jealousy.

द्वेष्टाह्यसुखमादत्तेयथैवनिधनं तथा॥

dveṣṭāhyasukhamādatteyathaivanidhanaṃ tathā||

Jealousy makes a person unhappy, and is also fatal.

King Ḍhritaraśtra, Sabhā Parva Ch.50 V.01

CONTEXT:

Pursuant to their exile upon losing the game of dice with Kauravas, Pāṇḍava's enter the forest and start living there. Draupadī provokes Yudhiṣṭhira with her words and exhorts him to give up his forgiving nature. She questions him as to why he does not get angry remembering all the wrongs done to them by Kauravas, forcing them to live in forests far from the comforts of their Palace despite the valour of Bhīma, Arjuna, Nakula and Sahadeva. Draupadī reminds him of the teaching of King Prahlāda to his grandson Bali on the relative demerits of forgiveness when compared to the use of might. King Prahlāda spells out the pros and cons of forgiveness as well as the use of might. Hearing Draupadī exhorting him to choose path of might befitting the Kshatriyas (the Warrior class). In response Yudhiṣṭhira cites the virtues of forgiveness and the dire consequences which would visit the world if people are not forgiving.

क्षमाधर्मः क्षमायज्ञः क्षमावेदाःक्षमाश्रुतम्।
यस्तामेवं विजानाति ससर्वं क्षन्तुमर्हति॥

kṣamādharma ḥkṣamāyajñaḥ kṣamāvedāḥ kṣamāśrutam|
yastāmevaṃ vijānāti sasarvaṃ kṣantumarhati||

Forgiveness is Dharma, forgiveness is sacrifice, forgiveness is the quintessence of Vedas, forgiveness is the essence of Shruti. He who knows this is capable of forgiving everything.

Yudhiṣṭhira, Vana Parva Ch.30 V.36

क्षमाब्रह्म क्षमासत्यं क्षमाभूतं च भाविच।
क्षमातपः क्षमाशौचं क्षमयाचोद्‌तं जगत्॥

kṣamābrahma kṣamāsatyaṃ kṣamābhūtaṃ ca bhāvi ca|
kṣamātapaḥ kṣamāśaucaṃ kṣamayācoddhṛtaṃ jagat||

Forgiveness is creator, forgiveness is truth, forgiveness is past and the future. Forgiveness is penance, forgiveness is purity, forgiveness sustains the universe.

Yudhiṣṭhira, Vana Parva Ch.30 V.37

CONTEXT:

Draupadī during the period of exile speaks to Yudhiṣṭhira about three causes that determine what a person achieves or fails to achieve in life. Firstly, Good or bad karma in past birth; Secondly, Destiny or Chance; thirdly, Efforts in the present. She says that a person should take recourse to Efforts in the present and not despair if they do not meet with success inspite of best of efforts, as success is dependent on various other circumstances known and unknown. But success cannot be achieved without efforts for sure. In this context she says that inspite of effort if one does not meet with success, one should not despair or indulge in self-deprecation. A person who indulges in self-deprecation would never earn prosperity.

न चैवात्मावमन्तव्यःपुरुषेण कदाचन।
न ह्यात्मपरिभूतस्य भूतिर्भवति भारत॥

Na caivātmāvamantavyaḥ puruṣeṇa kadācana|
na hyātmaparibhūtasya bhūtirbhavati bhārata||

No person should ever belittle himself, for the person who belittles himself never obtains prosperity.

Draupadī, Vana Parva Ch.33 V.54

CONTEXT:

In the vana parva several anecdotal narratives on various aspects of life and challenges faced by human beings previously and how they were overcome are presented through Rishis who visit the Pāṇḍava. One such narrative is popularly known as Nalopakhyana Parva, the story of King Nala and Queen Damayantī. King Nala loses his kingdom in a game of dice and has to go to forest and there he abandons his wife Damayantī, hoping that at least she can go back to her parent's palace and live comfortably. She does reach her parent's palace and then sends emissaries to locate her husband by sending a encrypted poetic message which only her husband could decipher. She comes to know that a charioteer in King Rituparṇa's kingdom has decoded it and gave a reply. Queen Damayanti knowing for sure her husband is staying there as a charioteer sends a message announcing her decision to take another husband and invites King Rituparna for her Swayamvara (ancient Indian princess had the choice of selecting their husband amongst various princes who were invited to the assembly). The Swayamvara is announced one day later, knowing well that only King Nala could cover the distance in one day with his exceptional skills as a charioteer. King Rituparna requests Nala to take him to the swayamvara, Nala is confused to hear the news of his wife announcing a Swayamvara and consoles himself by thinking that she believes him to be dead.

King Rituparṇa during journey demonstrates his expertise in computing to Nala while appreciating the skills of Nala in handling horses. Nala requests him to teach him the game of dice and inturn offers to share his knowledge about horses. King Rituparna observes that knowledge in all branches is not present in any one person.

सर्वः सर्वं न जानाति सर्वज्ञो नास्ति कश्चन।
नैकत्र परिनिष्ठास्ति ज्ञानस्य पुरुषे क्वचित्॥

sarvaḥ sarvaṃ na jānāti sarvajño nāsti kaścana|
naikatra pariniṣṭhāsti jñānasya puruṣe kvacit||

Everything is not known to everyone. There is no one who is versed in all subjects. Knowledge in all subjects is not found in any one person.

King Rituparna Vana Parva Ch.70 V.08

CONTEXT:

Pursuant to their exile after losing game of dice with Kauravas, Pāṇḍava enter the forest and start living there. Draupadī provokes Yudhiṣṭhira with her words and exhorts him to give up his nature to be forgiving. She questions him as to why he does not get angry remembering all the wrongs done to them by Kauravas, forcing them to live in forests far from the comforts of their Palace despite the valour of Bhīma, Arjuna, Nakula and Sahadeva. Draupadī cites the conversation between King Prahlāda with his grandson Bali, wherein King Prahlāda highlights various virtues including that of Humility.

मृदुनामार्दवं हन्ति मृदुना हन्ति दारुणम्।
नासाध्यं मृदुना किञ्चित्तस्मात्तीक्ष्णतरोमृदुः॥

mṛdunāmārdavaṃ hanti mṛdunā hanti dāruṇam|
nāsādhyaṃ mṛdunā kiñcittasmāttīkṣṇataromṛduḥ||

Humility conquers the mighty and the weak, nothing is impossible for one who is humble.

King Prahlāda, Vana Parva Ch.29 V.30

CONTEXT:

The Pāṇḍava's on completing the period of 12 years in forest and one year incognito as per the condition of wager in the game of dice consult with their well-wishers on their future course of action. Knowing about this Ḍhritaraśtra sends his trusted emissary Sanjaya to the Pāṇḍava's with an advice not to take any hasty steps. Sanjaya returns to Hastināpura and meets Ḍhritaraśtra and chides him for his blind love for his son and takes leave of the King stating the message of Yudhisthra shall be delivered next day in the Kuru Assembly. Ḍhritaraśtra becomes restless wondering what the message carried by Sanjaya could be, which he did not disclose in private. Having become sleepless and burning from inside he calls his Counsel Vidura and shares with him about his sleeplessness and requests Vidura to speak to him about what would be conducive for a man who is suffering from sleeplessness and is burning from inside. Ḍhritaraśtra requests Vidura to speak to him about things which would enlighten his mind and reduce his anxiety. Vidura then gives a discourse which is popularly known as ViduraNīti (Vidura's moral prescriptions).

यथा मधुसमादत्ते रक्षन्पुष्पाणि षट्पदः।
तद्वदर्थान्मनुष्येभ्य आदद्यादविहिंसया॥

Yathā madhusamādatte rakṣanpuṣpāṇi ṣaṭpadaḥ|
tadvadarthānmanuṣyebhya ādadyādavihiṃsayā||

Just as a Honeybee extracts honey from a flower, so should tax be collected from people without harming them.

Vidura, Udyoga Parva Ch.34 V.17

अनारभ्याभवन्त्यर्थाः केचिन्नित्यं तथागताः।
कृतः पुरुषकारोऽपि भवेद्येषु निरर्थकः॥

anārabhyābhavantyarthāḥ kecinnityaṃ tathāgatāḥ|
kṛtaḥ puruṣakāro'pi bhavedyeṣu nirarthakaḥ||

One should not start something which cannot be completed and would render the efforts futile.

Vidura, Udyoga Parva Ch.34 V.20

सत्येन रक्ष्यते धर्मो विद्या योगेनरक्ष्यते।
मृजया रक्ष्यते रूपं कुलं वृत्तेन रक्ष्यते॥

Satyena rakṣyate dharmo vidyā yogena rakṣyate|
mṛjayā rakṣyate rūpaṃ kulaṃ vṛttena rakṣyate||

Truth protects Dharma, Knowledge is preserved by practice. Grooming takes care of looks and the clan is preserved by occupation.

Vidura, Udyoga Parva Ch.34 V.37

शीलं प्रधानं पुरुषेतद्यस्येह प्रणश्यति।
नतस्य जीवितेनार्थोन धनेन न बन्धुभिः॥

śīlaṃ pradhānaṃ puruṣetadyasyeha praṇaśyati|
natasya jīvitenārthona dhanena na bandhubhiḥ||

Character is primary for a person. Having wealth and friends is meaningless for one devoid of character.

Vidura, Udyoga Parva Ch.34 V.46

तृणोल्कयाज्ञायतेजातरूपं, युगेभद्रोव्यवहारेणसाधुः।
शूरोभयेष्वर्थकृच्छ्रेषुधीरः, कृच्छ्रास्वापत्सुसुहृदश्चारयश्च॥

tṛṇolkayājñāyatejātarūpaṃ,
yugebhadrovyavahāreṇasādhuḥ|
śūrobhayeṣvarthakṛcchreṣudhīraḥ,
kṛcchrāsvāpatsusuhṛdaścārayaśca||

Gold is tested by fire, one of good upbringing by his behavior, an honest person by his conduct. A brave person is tested in times of fear, a self-controlled person in times of poverty and friends and enemies during adversity and vulnerability.

Vidura, Udyoga Parva Ch.35 V.42

जरारूपं हरति हि धैर्यमाशा, मृत्युः प्राणान्धर्मचर्यामसूया।
क्रोधः श्रियं शीलमनार्यसेवा, ह्रियंकामः सर्वमेवाभिमानः॥

jarārūpaṃ harati hi dhairyamāśā,
mṛtyuḥ prāṇāndharmacaryāmasūyā|
krodhaḥ śriyaṃ śīlamanāryasevā,
hriyaṃkāmaḥ sarvamevābhimānaḥ||

Decrepitude destroys beauty, fear destroys hope, death destroys life, envy destroys virtue, anger destroys prosperity, associations with lowly destroys good behavior, lust destroys modesty and ego destroys everything.

Vidura, Udyoga Parva Ch.35 V.43

यस्मिन्यथा वर्तते यो मनुष्यस्तस्मिंस्तथा वर्तितव्यं स धर्मः।
मायाचारो मायया वर्तितव्यः साध्वाचारः साधुना प्रत्युदेयः॥

Yasminyathā vartate yo manuṣyastasmiṃstathā vartitavyaṃ sa dharmaḥ|
Māyācāro māyayā vartitavyaḥ,
sādhvācāraḥ sādhunā pratyudeyaḥ||

One ought to behave towards another having regard to how the other person behaves with him; this is consistent with Dharma. One may behave deceitfully with a person who is deceitful, but ought to be honest, with the person who is honest.

Vidura, Udyoga Parva Ch.37 V.07

त्यजेत्कुलार्थे पुरुषं ग्रामस्यार्थेकुलंत्यजेत्।
ग्रामं जनपदस्यार्थे आत्मार्थे पृथिवींत्यजेत्॥

Tyajetkulārthe puruṣaṃ grāmasyārthe kulaṃtyajet|
grāmaṃ janapadasyārthe ātmārthe pṛthivīṃ tyajet||

An individual may be sacrificed for the clan, a clan may be sacrificed for the village. A village may be sacrificed for a Nation and entire earth may be sacrificed for 'Ātmā'.

Vidura, Udyoga Parva Ch.37 V.16

द्वेष्यो न साधुर्भवति न मेधावी न पण्डितः।
प्रियेशुभानिकर्माणिद्वेष्येपापानिभारत॥

dveṣyo na sādhurbhavati na medhāvī na paṇḍitaḥ|
priyeśubhānikarmāṇi dveṣye pāpāni bhārata||

One who hates someone, does find the one so hated neither intelligent nor knowledgeable. While, one tends to attribute to him whom he likes everything good, and one whom he hates everything bad.

Vidura, Udyoga Parva Ch.39 V.04

कान्तारवनदुर्गेषु कृच्छ्रास्वापत्सु संभ्रमे।
उद्यतेषु च शस्त्रेषु नास्ति शेषवतां भयम्॥

kāntāravanadurgeṣu kṛcchrāsvāpatsu saṃbhrame|
udyateṣu ca śastreṣu nāsti śeṣavatāṃ bhayam||

Amidst deserts, or dense forests, or inaccessible fortresses, in the midst of deadly weapons upraised for striking him, he that has the strength of mind entertains no fear.

Vidura, Udyoga Parva Ch.39 V.53

CONTEXT:

Sanjaya narrates to Ḍhritarāśtra that Bhīṣma had fallen in the battle. In angst, Ḍhritarāśtra blames Duryodhana for causing sorrow to him. Sanjaya decries Ḍhritarāśtra for blaming Duryodhana for the sorrow caused to him.

य आत्मनो दुश्चरिताद शुभं प्राप्नुयान्नरः।
एनसातेननान्यं स उपाशङ्कितुमर्हति॥

ya ātmano duścaritāda śubhaṃ prāpnuyānnaraḥ|
enasātenanānyaṃ sa upāśaṅkitumarhati||

The man, who incurs evil as the consequence of his own wrongdoing, should not blame others for his own failings.

Sanjaya, Bhīṣma Parva Ch.16 V.02

CONTEXT:

Bhīṣma while lying on the bed of arrows instructs Yudhiṣṭhira on various branches of learning. The instructions are in the form of questions and answers with anecdotal references to events in the past to make it easy to understand. Yudhiṣṭhira asks which amongst friends/relatives, Karma, Wealth, or Wisdom should be the refuge of a person. Bhīṣma replies with this verse.

प्रज्ञा प्रतिष्ठा भूतानां प्रज्ञा लाभः परोमतः।
प्रज्ञा नैःश्रेयसी लोके प्रज्ञा स्वर्गोमतः सताम्॥

prajñā pratiṣṭhā bhūtānāṃ prajñā lābhaḥparomataḥ|
praj ñānaiḥśreyasī loke prajñā svargomataḥsatām||

Wisdom is a matter of honor or is highly honored by creatures. Wisdom is considered as the greatest of acquisitions. Wisdom is the greatest happiness in the world. Wisdom is regarded as heaven by the good and virtuous.

Bhīṣma, Śānti Parva Ch.173 V.2

CONTEXT:

Bhīṣma while lying on the bed of arrows instructs Yudhiṣṭhira on various branches of learning. The instructions are in the form of questions and answers with anecdotal references to events in the past to make it easy to understand. Yudhiṣṭhira laments seeing his grandfather lying on a bed of arrows and seeks his guidance to cleanse his sins which caused, the grandsire to lay on the bed of arrows. Bhīṣma consoles him and narrates the anecdote of an old Lady Gautami, whose young son dies of a snake bite. Seeing her suffer in grief on the untimely death of her son, a hunter named Arjunaka catches hold of the snake and seeks to avenge the death of her son by killing the snake. Gautami rebukes Arjunaka and states that the inevitable cannot be undone and there is no purpose in committing a sin by seeking retribution. The conversation is very subtle interpretation on who is responsible for the untimely death of a young man the Snake or Death or Time or Karma. In the final analysis the real cause of untimely death of the young man is found to be his own karma. The interesting discourse brings out the subtilities which calm an agitated mind to find solace in karma philosophy.

प्लवन्ते धर्मलघवो लोकेऽम्भसि यथा प्लवाः।
मज्जन्ति पापगुरवः शस्त्रं स्कन्नमिवोदके॥

plavante dharmalaghavo loke'mbhasi yathā plavāḥ|
majjanti pāpaguravaḥ śastraṃ skannamivodake||

Those that have made themselves weightless by the practice of virtuous deeds, manage to cross the sea of this world as a ship crosses the ocean. But those that have made themselves heavy with sin sink to the bottom, like an arrow thrown in water.

Gautami, Anuśāsana Parva, Ch.01 V.15

CONTEXT:

Bhīṣma while lying on the bed of arrows instructs Yudhiṣṭhira on various branches of learning. The instructions are in the form of questions and answers with anecdotal references to events in the past to make it easy to understand. Yudhiṣṭhira asks about parity between son and daughter in the context of inheritance. Bhīṣma says that son is one's own self, and the daughter is like the son.

सा हि पुत्रसमा राजन्विहिता कुरुनन्दन॥

sā hi putrasamā rājanvihitā kurunandana||

The daughter has been ordained to be equal to the son.

Bhīṣma, Anuśāsana Parva Ch.47 V.25

CONTEXT:

Bhīṣma while lying on the bed of arrows instructs Yudhiṣṭhira on various branches of learning. The instructions are in the form of questions and answers with anecdotal references to events in the past to make it easy to understand. Yudhiṣṭhira seeks instructions from Bhīṣma as to who deserve to be worshipped and respected. Bhīṣma states that he reveres persons who have knowledge of Ātmā and those who make gifts to the learned without pride.

ये चापि सततं राजस्तेषां च स्पृहयाम्यहम्।
शक्यं ह्येवाहवे योद्‌ध न दातुमनसूयितम्॥

ye cāpisatatamṛājamsteṣāṃ ca spṛhayāmyaham|
śakyaṃ hyevāhave yoddhuṃ na dātumanasūyitam||

It is easy to fight in the battle, but not so to make a gift without pride or vanity.

Bhīṣma, Anuśāsana Parva, Ch.08. V.9, 10

Chapter 11

Mental Health

CONTEXT:

Sanjaya on seeing Ḍhritaraśtra being anxious after the Pāṇḍava have left for forest asks him why he is anxious after obtaining the entire wealth of the Pāṇḍava. Ḍhritaraśtra says that anyone who shall have to face the Pāṇḍava's in the battlefield is bound to be anxious. Sanjaya reminds him of the advice of Bhīṣma, Droṇāacharya and Vidura against the game of dice between Kauravas and Pāṇḍava. Having ignored their advice. Kauravas have brought upon the calamity by their actions. Adverse time make a person see things differently than what they really are. Understanding is polluted by sin and good appears to be evil and evil appears to be good.

न कालोदण्डमुद्यम्यशिरः कृन्ततिकस्यचित्।
कालस्य बलमेतावद्विपरीतार्थ दर्शनम्॥

na kālodaṇḍamudyamyaśiraḥ kṛntatikasyacit|
kālasya balametāvadviparītārtha darśanam||

The time that brings on destruction does not come with an upraised stick and smash one's head. Time makes one see the opposite, i.e, evil in good and good in evil.

Sanjaya, Sabhā Parva Ch.72 V.11

CONTEXT:

Unable to provide proper food and hospitality for the Brahmanas who were following Pāṇḍava in forest, Yudhiṣṭhira is distressed and expresses his angst for not being in a position to provide the hospitality they deserve. He requests them to return to Hastināpura, Śaunaka, a Brāhmaṇa well versed in Knowledge of Self and Sānkhya system of Yoga, counsels Yudhiṣṭhira on the ill effects of mental stress.

मानसेन हिदुःखेन शरीरमुपतप्यते।
अयःपिण्डेन तप्तेन कुम्भ संस्थमिवोदकम्॥

mānasena hiduḥkhena śarīramupatapyate|
ayaḥpiṇḍena taptena kumbha saṃsthamivodakam||

Mental stress leads to physical ailments, similar to how calm water tends to boil when in contact with a hot metal.

Śaunaka – a Brāhmaṇa, Vana Parva Ch.02 V.24

मानसंशमयेत्तस्माज्ज्ञानेनाग्निमिवाम्बुना।
प्रशान्तेमानसेदुःखे शारीरमुपशाम्यति॥

mānasaṃśamayettasmājjñānenāgnimivāmbunā|
praśāntemānaseduḥkhe śārīramupaśāmyati||

Mental stress is dispelled by true knowledge, as water douses fire. Once the mind is at ease the body also recuperates.

Saunaka – a Brahmana, Vana Parva Ch.02 V.25

CONTEXT:

The Pāṇḍava on completing the period of 12 years in forest and one year incognito, as per the condition of wager in the game of dice, consult with their well-wishers on their future course of action. After hearing Knowing about this Ḍhritaraśtra sends his trusted emissary Sanjaya to the Pāṇḍava with an advice not to take any hasty steps. Sanjaya returns to Hastināpura and meets Ḍhritaraśtra and chides him for his blind love for his son and takes leave of the King stating the message of King Yudhisthra shall be delivered next day in the Kuru Assembly. Ḍhritaraśtra becomes restless and unable to sleep wondering what the message could be carried by Sanjaya which he did not disclose in private. Having become sleepless and burning from inside he calls his advisor Vidura and informs him that he is experiencing sleeplessness and requests Vidura to speak to him about things which would be conducive for a man who is suffering from sleeplessness and is burning from inside. So that it would enlighten his mind and reduce his anxiety. Vidura then gives a discourse which is popularly known as ViduraNīti (Vidura's moral prescriptions).

अभियुक्तं बलवता दुर्बलं ही न साधनम्।
हृतस्वंकामिनंचोरमाविशन्ति प्रजागराः॥

abhiyuktaṃ balavatā durbalaṃ hī na sādhanam|
hratasvaṃkāminaṃcoramāviśanti prajāgarāḥ||

Sleeplessness is caused to one who is overwhelmed by the powerful, one who has failed in his endeavors, one who has lost his wealth, one who is burning with desire and a thief.

Vidura, Udyoga Parva Ch.33 V.13

तथैव योग विहितं न सिध्येत्कर्मयन्नृप।
उपाययुक्तंमेधावी न तत्रग्लपयेन्मनः॥

tathaivayogavihitaṃ na sidhyetkarmayannṛpa|
upāyayuktaṃmedhāvī na tatraglapayenmanaḥ||

When success is not achieved inspite of the application of fair and proper methods, an intelligent man does not grieve.

Vidura, Udyoga Parva Ch.34 V.07

यच्छक्यं ग्रसितुं ग्रस्यं ग्रस्तं परिणमेच्चयत्।
हितं च परिणामेयत्तदद्यं भूतिमिच्छता॥

yacchakyaṃ grasituṃ grasyaṃ grastaṃ pariṇameccayat|
hitaṃ ca pariṇāmeyattadadyaṃ bhūtimicchatā||

One who wishes to have good health and prosperity, should consume only such quantity that is easy to chew and digest.

Vidura, Udyoga Parva Ch.34 V.14

वनस्पतेरपक्कानिफलानिप्रचिनोतियः।
स नाप्नोतिरसं तेभ्यो बीजं चास्यविनश्यति॥

vanaspaterapakvāniphalānipracinotiyaḥ|
sa nāpnotirasaṃ tebhyo bījaṃ cāsyavinaśyati||

A person who plucks a fruit which is not yet ripe, not only fails to relish it but also destroys a fruit bearing seed.

Vidura, Udyoga Parva Ch.34 V.15

यस्तु पक्वमुपादत्तेकाले परिणतं फलम्।
फलाद्रसंसलभते बीजाच्चैव फलं पुनः॥

Yastu pakvamupādattekāle pariṇataṃ phalam|
phalādrasaṃsalabhate bījāccaiva phalaṃ punaḥ||

A person who waits for the fruit to ripen, enjoys the fruits, and also obtains a fruit bearing seed.

Vidura, Udyoga Parva Ch.34 V.16

संतापाद्भ्रश्यते रूपं संतापाद्भ्रश्यते बलम्।
संतापाद्भ्रश्यतेज्ञानं संतापाव्द्याधिमृच्छति॥

saṃtāpādbhraśyate rūpaṃ saṃtāpādbhraśyate balam|
saṃtāpādbhraśyatejñānaṃ saṃtāpāvdyādhimṛcchati||

Sorrow diminishes beauty; sorrow diminishes strength; sorrow diminishes understanding; sorrow brings disease.

Vidura, Udyoga Parva Ch.36 V.42

स्वास्तीर्णानिशयनानिप्रपन्ना, नवैभिन्नाजातुनिद्रां लभन्ते।
नस्त्रीषुराजन्रतिमाप्नुवन्तिनमागधैःस्तूयमानानसूतैः॥

svāstīrṇāniśayanāniprapannā, na
vaibhinnājātunidrāṃlabhante|
na strīṣurājanratimāpnuvanti na māgadhaiḥstūyamā nā
nasūtaiḥ||

They that are no longer in peace with their relatives, obtain no sleep even if they have access to well-made beds; nor do they, o King, derive any pleasure from women, or the laudatory hymns of bards and eulogists.

Vidura, Udyoga Parva Ch.36 V.53

बुद्ध्याभयंप्रणुदतितपसाविन्दतेमहत्।

buddhyābhayaṃpraṇudatitapasāvindatemahat|

Knowledge drives away fear, perseverance enables greatness.

Vidura, Udyoga Parva Ch.36 V.50

CONTEXT:

ŚriKṛṣṇa in his discourse popularly knows as Bhagavadīgtā spells out certain eternal truths. This discourse happens in the midst of two Armies ready to face each other in the battlefield of Kurukshetra. ŚriKṛṣṇa dispels the darkness which had taken over the mind of Arjuna and guides him with the light of knowledge.

उद्धरेदात्मनात्मानं नात्मानमवसादयेत्।
आत्मैव ह्यात्मनो बन्धुरात्मैवरिपुरात्मनः॥

uddharedātmanātmānaṃ nātmānamavasādayet|
ātmaiva hyātmano bandhurātmaivaripurātmanaḥ||

One should elevate himself by his own exertion and not denigrate himself. For, one is, his own friend and his own foe.

ŚriKṛṣṇa, Bhagavadīgtā, Bhīṣma Parva Ch.28 V.05

CONTEXT:

Bhīṣma while lying on the bed of arrows instructs Yudhiṣṭhira on various branches of learning. The instructions are in the form of questions and answers with anecdotal references to events in the past. Bhīṣma recalls the conversation between Indra who comes in the form of a jackal and Kaśyapa, a Learned Man. Kaśyapa is hit by a chariot and falls by the side of road in great pain, in angst, he contemplates giving up his life, for he thinks there is no value for his life being a poor man. Indra appears in the form of a jackal and advises him against the thought of giving up his life in despair. Indra reminds him that all creatures aspire for a human life, which is exceedingly difficult to obtain. Amongst men to be a learned man is even more difficult. Having obtained a human life, it should not be given up in folly.

अकार्यमिति चैवेमनात्मानं संत्यजाम्यहम्।
नेतः पापीयासीं योनिंपतेयमपरामिति॥

akāryamiti caivemamṃnātmānaṃ saṃtyajāmyaham|
netaḥ pāpīyāsīṃ yoniṃpateyamaparāmiti||

I do not renounce life because it is a very sinful act, and lest indeed, I may have a more miserable life in the next birth.

Bhīṣma, Śānti Parva Ch.173 V.20

मनुष्या ह्याढ्यतां प्राप्य राज्यमिच्छन्त्यनन्तरम्।
राज्याद्देवत्वमिच्छन्ति देवत्वादिन्द्रतामपि॥

manuṣyā hyāḍhyatāṃ prāpya rājyamicchantyanantaram|
rājyāddevatvamicchanti devatvādindratāmapi||

Having acquired riches men next wish for sovereignty. Having acquired sovereignty, they next wish to be gods. Having acquired the status of Gods, they then wish to be the king of the gods.

Bhīṣma, Śānti Parva, Ch.173 V.23

न तृप्तिः प्रियलाभेऽस्ति तृष्णा नाद्भिः प्रशाम्यति।
संप्रज्वलति सा भूयः समिद्भिरिवपावकः॥

na tṛptiḥpriyalābhe'sti tṛṣ ṇānādbhiḥpraśāmyati|
saṃprajvalati sā bhūyaḥ samidbhirivapāvakaḥ||

Contentment does not come from acquisition of objects of desire. The thirst for acquisition of material things increases with each new acquisition, as adding fuel to fire only increases the fire.

Bhīṣma, Śānti Parva, Ch.173 V.25

अस्त्येव त्वयि शोको वै हर्षश्चास्ति तथा त्वयि।
सुखदुःखे तथा चोभे तत्र का परिदेवना॥

Astyeva tvayi śoko vai harṣaścāsti tathā tvayi|
sukhaduḥkhe tathā cobhe tatra kā paridevanā||

Happiness and grief are one's companions for life. When both happiness and misery are within you, why should you yield to grief?

Bhīṣma, Śānti Parva, Ch.173 V.26

न खल्वप्यरसज्ञस्य कामः क्वचनः जायते।
संस्पर्शाद्दर्शनाद्वापि श्रवणाद्वापि जायते॥

na khalvapyarasajñasya kāmaḥ kvacanaḥ jāyate|
saṃsparśāddarśanādvāpi śravaṇādvāpi jāyate||

One who has not experienced the enjoyment of a certain object, never feels a desire for that object. Desire originates from the actual experience of the pleasure that touch, or sight, or hearing gives.

Bhīṣma, Śānti Parva, Ch.173 V.28

CONTEXT:

Bhīṣma while lying on the bed of arrows instructs Yudhiṣṭhira on various branches of learning. The instructions are in the form of questions and answers with anecdotal references to events in the past. Yudhiṣṭhira asks Bhīṣma, what kind of understanding does a King who lost his kingdom and crushed by time need to live on earth? In response Bhīṣma narrates the anecdote of Asura King Bali, son of Virocana. Indra finds Bali in an animal form and teases him for his current state deprived of his Kingdom. In response Bali explains how Time is immensely powerful, and those who know the transitory nature of time are not affected by the highs and lows of life. Bali speaks of eternal truth and why one should not indulge in vanity.

भूतानां निधनं निष्ठास्रोतसामिव सागरः।

bhūtānāṃ nidhanaṃ niṣṭhāstrotasāmiva sāgaraḥ|

As the destination of all rivers is the ocean, so the end of all embodied creatures is death.

Bali, Śānti Parva, Ch.217 V.9

कालः सर्वं समादत्ते कालः सर्वं प्रयच्छति।
कालेन विधृतं सर्वं मा कृथाः शक्र पौरुषम्॥

kālaḥ sarvaṃ samādatte kālaḥ sarvaṃ prayacchati|
kālena vidhṛtaṃ sarvaṃ mā kṛthāḥ śakra pauruṣam||

It is time that gives everything and again takes away everything. It is time that ordains all things. Do not, O shakra, brag of your valour.

Bali, Śānti Parva, Ch.217 V.25

Chapter 12

Power of Words

CONTEXT:

The Pāṇḍava's on completing the period of 12 years in forest and one year incognito, as per the condition of wager in the game of dice, consult with their well-wishers on their future course of action. After hearing knowing about this Ḍhritaraśtra sends his trusted emissary Sanjaya to the Pāṇḍava's with an advice not to take any hasty steps. Sanjaya returns to Hastināpura and meets Ḍhritaraśtra and chides him for his blind love for his son and takes leave of the King stating the message of King Yudhisthra shall be delivered next day in the Kuru Assembly. Ḍhritaraśtra becomes restless and unable to sleep wondering what the message could be carried by Sanjaya which he did not disclose in private. Having become sleepless and burning from inside he calls his advisor Vidura and informs him that he is experiencing sleeplessness and requests Vidura to speak to him about things which would be conducive for a man who is suffering from sleeplessness and is burning from inside. So that it would enlighten his mind and reduce his anxiety. Vidura then gives a discourse which is popularly known as ViduraNīti(Vidura's moral prescriptions).

संरोहति शरैर्विद्धं वनं परशुनाहतम्।
वाचादुरुक्तं बीभत्सं न संरोहति वाक्क्षतम्॥

saṃrohati śarairviddhaṃ vanaṃ paraśunāhatam|
vācāduruktaṃ bībhatsaṃ na saṃrohati vākkṣatam||

Forest cut down by axe grows back, but a heart pierced by harsh words seldom recovers.

Vidura, Udyoga Parva Ch.34 V.75

कर्णिनालीकनाराचानिर्हरन्ति शरीरतः।
वाक्शल्यस्तुननिर्हर्तुंशक्यो हृदिशयोहिसः॥

karṇinālīkanārācānirharanti śarīrataḥ|
vākśalyastunanirhartuṃśakyo hṛdiśayohisaḥ||

Arrows and daggers which pierce the body can be removed, but words which pierce one's heart cannot be removed.

Vidura, Udyoga Parva Ch.34 V.76

अभ्यावहतिकल्याणं विविधा वाक्सुभाषिता।
सैवदुर्भाषिताराजन्ननर्थायोपपद्यते॥

abhyāvahatikalyāṇaṃvividhāvāksubhāṣitā|
saivadurbhāṣitārājannanarthāyopapadyate||

Pleasant words bring about good, while spiteful words bring about unpleasant consequences.

Vidura, Udyoga Parva Ch.34 V.74

CONTEXT:

Part of ViduraNeeti – Vidura refers to the conversation between Ṛṣi Haṃsa (Son of Rishi Atri) with Gods. Gods beseech the Learned Rishi to give them a discourse on wisdom. Learned Rishi speaks of the virtues of not speaking harshly and treating both agreeable and disagreeable like his own self. He proclaims that even Gods seek the company of such man who even on being struck does not himself return the blow nor wishes slightest injury. He further exhorts virtues of speech and what is to be spoken.

अव्याहृतं व्याहृताच्छ्रेय आहुः, सत्यं वदेव्याहृतंतद्द्वितीयम्।
प्रियंवदेव्याहृतंतत्तृतीयं, धर्म्यं वदेव्याहृतं तच्चतुर्थम्॥

avyāhṛtaṃ vyāhṛtācchreyaāhuḥ,
satyaṃvadevdyāhṛtaṃtaddvitīyam|
priyaṃvadevdyāhṛtaṃtattṛtīyaṃ, dharmyaṃ
vadevdyāhṛtaṃ taccaturtham||

Silence, it is said, is better than speech; if one must speak, then speak the truth, if truth is to be spoken, it is better to speak what is agreeable; and if what is agreeable is to be said, then it is better to say what is consistent with Dharma.

ṚṣiHaṃsa (Son of ṚṣiAtri), Udyoga Parva Ch.36 V.12

Bibliography

a. Mahabharata in Sanskrit with English Translation, Volume-1 to 9, New Revised Edition: 2008 – M.N, Dutt, Parimal Publications.

b. V.S. Sukthankar's Mahabharata in Sanskrit

c. K.M. Ganguli's Mahabharata in English

d. Sanskrit Untranslatables by Rajiv Malhotra

e. Puranic Encyclopaedia – Vettam Mani Motilal Banarsidass Publishers

f. C. Rajgopalachari's – Bhagavadageeta